THE COLLEGE OF LAW
BS1 6HG
BRISTOL

Copyright in the Digital Age

Industry Issues and Impacts

D1322058

Edited by

TREVOR FENWICK

and

IAN LOCKS

The College of Law
of England and Wales

LIBRARY SERVICES

This Book is the Property of
THE COLLEGE OF LAW

INLP
Fen

The College of Law, Bristol

R00713

Copyright © 2010 The Stationers Company and the individual contributors
Cover photograph copyright © 2010 Derek Brown, Oblong Creative Ltd

Copyright in the Digital Age

British Library Cataloguing in Publication Data
A catalogue record for this book is available from the British Library

ISBN 9780854900800

Typeset in Optima and Palatino Linotype
Printed and bound in Great Britain by CPI Antony Rowe

Text published under the terms of the Creative Commons Attribution 3.0 Licence

You are free:
- to Share — to copy, distribute and transmit the work
- to Remix — to adapt the work

Under the following conditions:
- Attribution — You must attribute the work in the manner specified by the author or licensor (but not in any way that suggests that they endorse you or your use of the work).

With the understanding that:
- Waiver — Any of the above conditions can be waived if you get permission from the copyright holder.
- Public Domain — Where the work or any of its elements is in the public domain under applicable law, that status is in no way affected by the license.
- Other Rights — In no way are any of the following rights affected by the license:
  - Your fair dealing or fair use rights, or other applicable copyright exceptions and limitations;
  - The author's moral rights;
  - Rights other persons may have either in the work itself or in how the work is used, such as publicity or privacy rights.
- Notice — For any reuse or distribution, you must make clear to others the license terms of this work.

First published in 2010 by
Wildy, Simmonds & Hill Publishing
58 Carey Street
London WC2A 2JF
England

CONTENTS

ACKNOWLEDGEMENTS

The Stationers' Company is grateful to all those who have made this publication possible

The Editors

Trevor Fenwick is Managing Director of Euromonitor International, the leading data publisher of market research analysis and reference databases. He is Chairman of the Data Publishers Association and an ex-President of the European Association of Directory and Database Publishers.

Ian Locks, newspaper journalist and now a consultant to the publishing industry, was Chief Executive of magazine industry body PPA for 19 years until 2008, during which time he was a director of both the Publishers Licensing Society (PLS) and the Copyright Licensing Agency (CLA).

The Reviewers

Neville Cusworth was Chief Executive of the Butterworth Group 1987-99 and chairman 1990-99; he was a director of Reed Publishing Ltd 1989-93, and chairman of Butterworth-Heinemann Ltd 1990-93. He was Master Stationers Company 2006-07.

Dr. Sarah Thomas was appointed Bodley's Librarian and Director of Oxford University Library Services in February 2007. She is the first woman and non-British citizen to hold the position in 400 years. From 1996-2007 she was Cornell's University Librarian.

Clive Bradley started his career as a broadcaster and journalist, after reading for the bar (called 1961) at Cambridge and Yale. He was Chief Executive of The Publishers Association for 21 years and he continues to convene CICI. He is a specialist in copyright and employment law.

Editorial advice

Noel Osborne, specialist publisher, helped revive dormant publishing house, Phillimore, as editorial and production director in 1968, becoming managing director in 1992, and chairman in 2006. Master of The Stationers' Company 2008/09 he has seen more than 2,000 titles through the press.

Publisher

Wildy, Simmonds and Hill Publishing

Brian Hill and Wildy, Simmonds and Hill for publishing *Copyright in the Digital Age*

Print Partner

Ralph Bell and CPI Anthony Rowe for printing of *Copyright in the Digital Age*

This book is based on the website developed by The Stationers' Company, in the 300th anniversary year of the Statute of Anne, to inform the debate on the future of copyright in the digital age. We believe that, while the rights of rightsowners need to evolve in line with the times, nevertheless copyright is still the bedrock on which creative industries are based. As you can read in the pages this book contains, that is about 10 percent of the UK economy: all based on a concept evolved through 153 years of effort by the Stationers' Company before being encapsulated in a visionary piece of legislation in the name of Queen Anne enacted in April 1710.

However we have not been constrained by any "Stationers' Company view" and have invited submissions from a wide range of opinion – and continue to do so.

The primary purpose of this book is to inform the debate on the future of copyright in the digital age: a professional resource for those seeking information on the importance and value of Copyright to the UK's Creative Industries and to promote understanding of the importance of those industries and their reliance on their ability to "own" intellectual property through copyright legislation.

The book contains articles and submissions by leading industry practitioners, lawyers and academics with practical experience of the importance of Copyright in the UK as well as those at the "sharp end" as publishers and producers. It reflects the challenges to be faced with the development of the digital usage of copyright material.

It will help to inform all who work in or have interest in the protection of intellectual property whether they be working as producers in the sector, as legislators, academics, professional commentators or as students.

The Encouragement of Learning

SARAH THOMAS

BODLEY'S LIBRARIAN AND DIRECTOR OF OXFORD UNIVERSITY
LIBRARY SERVICES

Sarah Thomas was appointed Bodley's Librarian and Director of Oxford University Library Services in February 2007. She is the first woman and non-British citizen to hold the position in 400 years. From 1996-2007 she was Cornell's University Librarian. Previously she was the Acting Director of Public Services and Collection Management and Director for Cataloging at the Library of Congress (1992-1996), Chief of the Technical Services Division at the National Agricultural Library (1984- 1992, and Manager of Library Coordination at the Research Libraries Group (1979-1983). She began her career at Harvard's Widener Library cataloguing German books and introducing Harvard to OCLC via the Computer-Based Cataloguing Section (1973-1975).

Thomas led in the establishment of the Program for Cooperative Cataloging at the Library of Congress, and has been active in scholarly communication initiatives. Under her direction the Cornell University Library was honoured with the ACRL Excellence in Academic Libraries award in 2002. Thomas received the Melvil Dewey Award from the American Library Association in 2007. She has also served as the President of the Association of Research Libraries. In 2009 she was selected to the Simmons College Alumni Achievement Award. In 2010 Smith College awarded her the Smith Medal for exemplifying in her life and work the true purpose of a liberal arts education. Also in 2010, under her leadership, the Bodleian Libraries were awarded the Queen's Anniversary Prize for the excellence of their collections and their efforts, along with six other cultural heritage entities of the University of Oxford, in widening access to their historic collections.

Thomas graduated from Smith College in 1970, received a Master of Science in library science from Simmons College in 1973, and a Ph.D. in German literature in 1983.

In 1709 the Statute of Anne, "An Act for the Encouragement of Learning by vesting the Copies of Printed Books in the Authors or purchasers of such Copies, during the Times therein mentioned", recognised intellectual and creative achievements as a form of property. The Statute is credited as the inception of the law of copyright.

In the centuries preceding the enactment, which took effect 300 years ago, in 1710, the invention of the printing press and its uptake had resulted in a radical rescaling of the ability to generate copies of written works. By 1600, as many as 200 million volumes had been printed, and the dissemination of ideas was of massive importance.

The resulting proliferation of books, pamphlets, and other documents was of political, religious, economic, and educational significance. In England, the Stationers' Company, founded in 1403 and chartered in 1557, has played a prominent role in the production of books. The Worshipful Company of Stationers and Newspaper Makers controlled the publication of books and inhibited the illegal copying of books by registering the owners of texts in their Register. Sir Thomas Bodley built a strong foundation for Oxford's Bodleian Library by establishing an agreement in 1610 for the right to receive one copy of every title entered in the Stationers' Register. A century later this provision was incorporated in the Act for the Encouragement of Learning.

Over the centuries the rights of authors, printers, publishers, libraries, and readers have been the subject of much debate and regulation. At times, laws and regulations came into being to control the flow of ideas and were a form of censorship. As the economic value of intellectual property became better understood, the importance of copyright to protect the investment of authors and the printers and publishers who contributed value to the finished product became a more integral part of the framework on which our society rests. In the 21st century, as knowledge creation has become a dominant form of wealth generation and has superseded manufacturing as the leading industry, asserting ownership of intellectual property has become even more important than in the past.

In earlier times, the duration of the period in which a work remained under copyright was more limited. In the Statute of Anne, owners of copyright enjoyed an exclusive right to publish their work for 14 years with the possibility of extending copyright for a further 14 years, after which the work entered the public domain. This period of exclusivity has been lengthened in various amendments to copyright legislation, most recently in the UK in 1995 to 70 years after the death of the author for literary, dramatic, musical, or artistic works.

The ability to assert ownership, however, is tested by new modes of dissemination which elude easy control. In the digital age, the difference between a copy and original is often moot. The internet offers seemingly limitless possibilities to share content without copyright owners receiving compensation for the use of their property. The lengthening of time before which a work enters the public domain, the ease with which digital copies can be created and shared, and the intense struggle of commercial publishers of printed publications to remain viable in the internet era have resulted in copyright being one of the defining issues of contemporary times.

The stakes are high. Authors are intent on the goals of being fairly compensated for their creative work, having their works read and having their ideas and thoughts influence the future direction of knowledge and society. Publishers see not only their traditional livelihood challenged, but also the very core of their profession, in which they contribute to the success of the author and work through editing, other quality control measures, marketing, and distribution. Librarians find that their traditional role is squeezed on multiple fronts as the cost of acquiring publications rises at a rate far higher than their parent organisations are prepared to subsidize and as their readers migrate in droves to the digital world in which seamless and instantaneous access to all information is an expectation of growing proportions of users.

Google's strategy to digitise whole libraries and to organise and make available the world's information has drawn battlelines in the copyright wars. Other social networking and peer-to-peer sites for sharing music, video, and other creative works have been in the news and the courts as rights owners, new media companies, and users square off over access to information in society. A centuries-long debate over what should be freely available to encourage learning and the creation of new knowledge and what should be controlled to protect the rights of those who have generated, enhanced, and distributed the products of knowledge, in whatever physical manifestation, continues today in a lively and spirited manner. The essays contained in this publication reflect the various facets of these debates. Contributed by publishers, librarians, academics, guardians of copyright law, and others with an interest in the outcome of the debate, they represent a diverse spectrum of views. They will advance the interpretation of these important issues.

Central tension in copyright law.

The Stationers' Company and Copyright: a brief introduction

NOEL OSBORNE

Noel Osborne read Classics and History at Cambridge, and has been a specialist publisher of British local, family and corporate history for more than forty years. In 1968 he was instrumental in reviving the dormant publishing house, Phillimore, as editorial and production director for twenty years, before taking over as managing director in 1992, and chairman in 2006. He has personally seen through the press more than two thousand titles, including a modern, county-by-county translation of Domesday Book, and many Livery Company histories.

He was cloathed as a Liveryman of The Stationers' Company in 1974, and served as Master for 2008/09.

Stationers' Hall lies at the historic heart of the British printing and publishing industries. Names such as Paternoster Row – the lane which ran from Amen Corner through St Paul's Churchyard to what is now St Paul's Underground Station – resonate with anyone who examines imprints and verso title pages.

How did all this come about? It was no accident that the early members of our guild, formed in 1403, practised their craft or 'mistery' close to St Paul's Cathedral. These text-writers, limners and 'other good citizens of London who also bind and sell books' were producing and selling their handmade books for a market that was overwhelmingly clerical. They operated – unlike itinerant traders – from fixed, 'stationary' stands. Hence our name: Stationers.

This Guild was incorporated as the Company of Stationers of London by the royal Charter – granted by Philip of Spain and Mary Tudor – of 4 May 1557. The significance of a charter at that time can be appreciated when we recognise that, in the intervening century and a half since the formation of the Guild, two seismic shocks had marked the beginning of our modern world: first, the introduction of printing into England in 1476 made it possible to produce books for a mass, lay audience. Secondly, the Reformation brought in new ways of thinking.

As in all good business, there was something in it for both sides: the Crown and The Stationers' Company. While the Company feared the opportunity for piracy that mass production offered, the Charter, in effect, provided the Crown with an agent, as Mary realised that previous attempts to impose royal control on every new publication had failed. The Company was expected to find a way to stem the constant flow of seditious and heretical books. This could be dangerous territory: the Stationers' Charter was granted by a Catholic queen, but its confirmation two years later was by Protestant Elizabeth.

So, in addition to the normal rights afforded to a company, two specific privileges obtained by the Stationers on their own terms are enshrined in our Charter:

Firstly, exclusivity. No-one in the realm should act as a printer unless he were a Freeman of the Stationers' Company of London. Secondly, the Master and Wardens had the right to search the houses and business premises of all printers, bookbinders and booksellers in the kingdom, and to 'seize, take, hold, burn' anything printed without proper qualification, or who resisted the search. A Decree of 1566 strengthened this power still further by giving the Wardens the right to enter warehouses at ports and to examine any bales suspected of containing books. From the 1560s, therefore, a form of copyright could be secured by two methods: by royal Letters Patent; or by our Guild rule that made it an offence not to present to the Wardens – to put on record, as in the text 'Entered at Stationers' Hall' – every publication not protected by royal privilege. Even our short-lived Charter of 1684 includes royal approval of our 'publick Register'. Thus were printers and booksellers, if not authors or translators, safeguarded. This simple form of copyright protection was, as the historian Cyprian Blagden puts it, 'for about 350 years, in the eyes of the English-speaking world, the raison d'etre of the Stationers' Company.'

Indeed, by 1610 the Company had signed an Agreement with Sir Thomas Bodley to deposit a copy of every new book in the University Library at Oxford: this would be a feature of all future copyright control. It would be wrong to pretend that the system worked smoothly. The Company suffered innumerable problems with the protection of copyright, the conflicts between printers and booksellers, wholesalers and retailers, and with the unworkable Printing Act which lapsed forever in April 1695, while itself regularly defaulting on the deposit of new books in the Bodleian Library.

The first Copyright Act of 1709[1] gave the Stationers the maximum of theoretical authority and the minimum of practical power. Nonetheless, Copyright is the unique strand of overwhelming importance within the Stationers' Company. When the Copyright Act of 1911 came into force on 1 July 1912 it brought to an end the practice of record-keeping which the Stationers of the 16th century invented for their mutual protection, which Parliament adopted and modified through a series of Acts over two centuries, and which in modern times has given the Company a unique piece of international fame: the invention of copyright.

---

[1] The 1709 Statute of Anne, "An Act for the Encouragement of Learning by vesting the Copies of Printed Books in the Authors or purchasers of such Copies, during the Times therein mentioned", took effect on 10 April 1710.

Copyright and the Information Explosion: an Overview

CLIVE BRADLEY

Clive Bradley started his career as a broadcaster and journalist, after reading for the bar (called 1961) at Cambridge and Yale. He was broadcasting officer for the Labour Party and broadcasting adviser to Harold Wilson for the 1964 General Election, and after periods as a producer at the BBC and as a political journalist, he became a Group Labour Adviser to IPC, then the largest publishing and printing company in the western world, Deputy General Manager of the Daily and Sunday Mirror and then a director of The Observer, responsible for establishing new in-house production arrangements after the termination of the printing contract with The Times and for securing cost-effective manning levels.

After compiling the Newspaper Publishers Association's evidence to the Royal Commission on the Press in 1976, he held the appointment of Chief Executive of The Publishers Association for 21 years, supervising the association's work on promoting the market for books in domestic and export markets, the introduction of new publishing, production and distribution technologies, the enforcement and development of copyright and other legal issues, relationships with the European Commission, etc. In 1984, at the invitation of the Cabinet Office, he helped establish a new informal grouping (the Confederation of Information Communication Industries, or CICI) to give the leading content industries in broadcasting, publishing, music, video and software a more united and effective voice to the authorities in the digital age. He currently continues to convene CICI and arrange meetings with ministers and other authorities on convergency issues. He is a specialist in copyright and employment law.

Abstract: The problem of how to reward and secure a livelihood for authors and other creative workers, and the producers who develop and put their often speculative products on the market, when the output is ephemeral and easily copied without reward or compensation, is of fundamental importance as societies develop and rely more and more on creative input for their economic and social growth. The established system, *copyright,* accepted internationally, enables rights in creative works to be traded profitably and with proper returns to their creators by providing that the creator has the exclusive right to make or authorise the making of copies.

The digital revolution, with its ease of collecting vast archives of content which can be readily accessed and copied in quantity without loss of quality, in private and outside the control of the originator, has put the copyright system in doubt, making it difficult to enforce and encouraging wholesale illegal access and copying. How to develop the system to meet the new challenges is a matter of considerable controversy.

In this article, Clive Bradley gives an overview of the role and scope of copyright and discusses the main issues which arise in the digital environment, as an introduction to the contributions from leading experts.

1. The creative dilemma

Over the centuries, society has tried to find effective ways of rewarding its creative workers ('creators') – writers, visual artists, composers, performers, film makers, broadcasters, designers, writers of software, and the producers who develop creative works for the market – as deserving of proper return for the use of their talent, labour and investment, and to encourage them to make their output ('works') available to potential users for communal benefit. In this way, one person's creativity, knowledge, skill and investment foster new creativity, knowledge, skill and investment in creative works, the growth of human knowledge. The problem is that by its nature, creative output is ephemeral, easily copied and plagiarised by others, and so difficult to 'trade' on a viable basis of proper return to the creator. *Copyright* – the tradable right to control and 'sell' the authority to make copies of works originated by the creator - is the internationally accepted means of engineering this – a form of 'intellectual property' vested in the creator, along with patents and trademarks – an asset accruing to the creator.

The economic and social value of this output is immense, though insufficiently recognised. It is estimated that, in the UK at the beginning of the 21st century, the creative industries, including publishing, broadcasting, music, film, design and software, contribute something of the order of £150bn to the UK economy annually – approaching 10% of total GDP. They also offer the best prospect of any UK industry for future growth and have significant export markets – a world leader.

This enterprise has been thrown into sharp relief over the past 20 years by the dramatic emergence of sophisticated digital information technology and the internet, creating vastly more powerful means of storing, accessing and copying creative works, enabling accurate and multiple copies of creative works to be made outside the control of their creators, providing significant benefits in terms of access to information, but threatening the ability of creators to obtain a fair return from their work and the viability of the systems which produce valuable creative works for the benefit of users. For many parts of the creative sector, these developments are seen as threatening their future existence, and at the very least they involve massive changes in the ways in which vital creative materials become available to users and by which creative workers are able to maintain their livelihood.

These developments, often described as a paradigm shift in the production and use of creative works, has been the subject of intense worldwide study, broadly concluding that the protection of the intellectual property which underlies creative endeavour is vital and itself confers major benefits, but not offering clear ways forward.

This 'digital revolution' has resulted in a major division of opinion about the future of the systems to protect and support the exercise of creative rights in copyright. One school of thought, primarily represented by the creative community, argues that copyright remains a sustainable regime for the future, needing only some tweaking to deal with new issues and effective enforcement, while another argues that copyright as it has existed is unworkable in the new, consumer-led, digital environment, standing in the way of digital technology and the ability of users to benefit from the technology. Both sides accept that new 'business models' have to be developed by the creative community if it is to have a sustainable future: the argument is how best to make these new models work. While the latter argument has the advantage of seeming 'modern' and on the side of new technologies, and the former can seem luddite, the creative industries are *not* trying to destroy the uses of the digital technology, but to find ways of maintaining viable systems *using* the technology, with copyright, which has regularly developed over the years to meet modern needs, providing a sound base.

A new paradigm shift

If the technological developments over the past 20 years have been dramatic, a further paradigm shift is now in progress. Before the 21st century, the basic use of new digital technology was dependent on the personal computer, with the user able to access creative content from new digital media, such as discs and then the internet, and to exchange information through computer networks. This was revolutionary enough, but the 21st century has seen the development of complex but inexpensive devices, initially in 2001 the IPod (a hand-held device loaded through the PC), providing access to music through the Apple ITunes store, revolutionising the music market. ITunes and similar systems generally operate within established copyright law, but run alongside illicit file-sharing services enabling massive unpaid-for copying between users. Then in 2009 came new wireless devices which enabled users to download content, in particular e-books and e-periodicals, and potentially newspapers and much more, into increasingly attractive hand-held devices, with formats similar to those of the 'old' technology, without the mediation of a PC, wherever they happened to be – e-readers.

Potentially this latest development may mark the next stage of the digital revolution, enabling producers – not just the established media – to dispense with the expensive 'old' technology of printing presses and physical distribution and publish only digital works distributed digitally. This throws into relief the need to ensure effective trading mechanisms of the kind protected by copyright. Unfortunately, perhaps, many producers of content in all parts of the creative industries were slow to establish such mechanisms, partly because the new systems needed to operate alongside the old, but also because the new systems were perceived as offering promotional benefits for the 'old' products which made charging for digital content unnecessary. This created an expectation on the part of the market that much content would be free (or largely paid for by advertisement revenue, not at the point of use), and it is only in the past few years that producers of many content products have adopted new, commercial, policies of charging for content on the internet. Even this is subject to well-informed doubters who do not accept that these new policies can be made to work.

The most recent example of a change in policy is the decision by News International to charge for access to its newspapers in digital form, initially *The Times* and *The Sunday Times*, either on the basis of weekly, monthly or annual subscriptions, or by bundling digital access in with subscriptions to the printed newspapers.

The development of digital, especially mobile, technology has also released a stampede of potential information providers, many of them less concerned with investing in *creating* content than in distributing information produced by others, creating a plethora of potential suppliers who expect to be able to distribute information without having to pay for the use of it and without having to charge for its use (gaining their own revenues from e.g. subscriptions to their own services or from advertisements displayed alongside the content), so creating an 'unlevel playing field' for fair competition.

Combined with the growth of social networks and blogs, enabling almost anyone to publish information and opinion, not all soundly based, and with well-resourced companies like Google operating vast search engines and seeking to digitise 'the whole of human knowledge', effectively becoming publishers of material they digitise, and with national libraries', sometimes in partnership with these commercial organisations, digitising their stocks and wanting to make their digital archive available, and with public libraries lending e-books as part of their free lending service, we face a situation of intense and often chaotic competition which raises important questions about the future of information and creative provision – not just systems of reward, but issues of privacy of personal data, quality and integrity of information and market dominance as well.

In April 2009, just before the General Election, Parliament passed the Digital Economy Act, offering potential tools which had been negotiated over many years to restrict illicit access over the internet to works in copyright and illicit file-sharing. At the current time, this project is in the course of development but its future implementation is unsure. In the USA the courts are considering an agreement between Google and the American publishing industry on a collective arrangement to permit Google to digitise in-copyright but out-of-print books which has raised concerns about the market power of Google and the position of authors, especially those based outside the USA.

The Stationers' Company Project

The Stationers' Company project, celebrating the tercentenary of the UK's first significant Copyright Act, the Act of Anne, 1709 (implemented in 1710), gathers together the analysis and opinions of authoritative experts on many of these new issues, and on the future of copyright law and creative industry practice, to create greater understanding and, hopefully, point towards effective solutions.

This prefatory article for the project seeks to give background to the role of copyright in our economic and social environment and to the issues that arise, and identifies some of the principal questions that are being debated. It is not a complete legal analysis but a guide to the operation of a system which has been seen as vital to the creative industries and to the effectiveness of 'information provision' generally.

2. Underlying problem of creative works

Over the ages, the problem has been that creative works are ephemeral and can be easily copied by persons other than their creator, without reward, and are of highly speculative value in the marketplace. Different models of reward have been used to support the makers of creative works in this uncertain segment of the economy, including, for creative workers, direct sale of copies, sale or licensing of the right to make copies, employment of the creator for salary or hire, and patronage, and, for producers, sale, subscription and advertising revenue. Where private sector activity has led to market deficiencies, these can be remedied by public funds, for example, the licence fee for the BBC (initially perhaps seen a means of maintaining control of a new medium, but now as a means of sustaining public service programming), the public and national library system, (initially to improve social mobility and now, like the NHS, often free for all at the point of use), and subsidy by, e.g. the Arts Council. Currently there is public discussion about how to overcome a newly perceived market deficiency, the continued provision of regional and local news which public funds may have to support.

The copyright solution

These models, important in themselves, need to be underwritten by law to sustain the vast variety of creative output that occurs and for which there is a market. For markets to work, there must be a viable commodity which can be traded. When a particular commodity, in this case creative works, can be readily copied and put on the market by parties who have not invested their skill and resources in it, the drive to generate creative works for the market becomes exhausted. Copyright makes creative works into a tradable commodity by giving the creator an exclusive right, enforceable at law, to make copies and trade in those copies: 'the trading system of works of the mind'.

This is generally accepted as a vital part of an effective society, as a matter of fact. *How* copyright is exercised may be debated, but that a creators' right in their original creations should exist is not. The only obvious alternative would be for the public sector to take financial responsibility for the creative sector, which is clearly unacceptable. Given the importance of creative works in economic and social society, it is imperative to have such a comprehensive system to enable fair rewards, reflecting the extent of use and the perceived value of the work, and giving creators the opportunity of earning a livelihood. The copyright owner may not need or wish to achieve financial reward: many works are created for purposes other than reward (for example this article), but the market option is available. It enables creative workers to prevent unauthorised people making copies of their works and to obtain reward from people authorised to make copies, or to assign or license the right to make copies to somebody else to exercise on their behalf, typically a publisher or producer (in this article referred to as the 'producer') who adds value to and markets the work.

Early origins of copyright

This necessity was recognised relatively crudely in Roman law and practice and in different forms of common law over the ages. In the UK, an embryonic right was introduced by the charter to the Stationers' Company in 1557, under which the Company (basically a guild of stationers, booksellers and printers) was granted the right (and duty) to seize unauthorised copies of books which its members had the sole right to print (and which were listed in its Register). Not surprisingly, the system also supported censorship and Guild monopoly which did not meet the needs of an emerging democratic society. However, the regime did point the way to a market- rather than paternalist-based economy for books, and began the growth of a competitive and innovative publishing industry, finding new authors and new markets at a time when the UK itself was undergoing enormous democratic and economic changes.

This system was augmented in 1709 by the Statute of Anne, which conferred limited exclusive rights on authors, through their printers, to print their books, and imposed penalties on persons who printed copies of books without authority. The Act was stated to be 'for the encouragement of learned men to compose and write useful books'. The new system stimulated a growing market and was developed and expanded over the years. More recently, the economic right was extended in the UK to include statutory authors' 'moral rights', basically the right to maintain integrity against distortion or false claims of authorship. The economic right can be separately traded for periods of time, type of reproduction (e.g. different editions of a book), and territory (usually different sovereign states), which enables authors and their publishers to optimise the exercise of their copyrights and to find innovative ways of taking creative works to market, including international markets.

The current statute in the UK is the Copyright, Designs and Patents Act 1988, which since then has been amended by Regulations, usually consequent upon EU or international directives or treaties.

Copyright law has been subject to many reports and reviews in recent years, to recommend changes needed to cope with new technologies, for example in the 1970s with widespread photocopying of books, periodicals and journals, and more recently, with the introduction of digital production and distribution of text, music, video, software and games. The most recent authoritative report is the *Gowers Review of Intellectual Property* (2006), which is still in the process of consultation and implementation, and which concluded that the copyright system basically worked well, and remained appropriate to the digital environment subject to various minor amendments.

Not a monopoly or restrictive practice

The copyright system, conferring an exclusive right to make and issue copies of an original work on the creator, is sometimes stigmatised as a monopoly or restrictive practice, so impacting itself on the rights of consumers. In law and practice, however, this is a misunderstanding of the nature of copyright. Copyright is an exclusive property right in a particular original work, no more a monopoly than other rights to property, and not preventing competition from similar but different original products aimed at the same market. 'Monopoly' only arises if a single producer has an over-dominant share of a market, as defined. Thus, it is possible to conceive of a monopoly in e.g. the market for children's books, but not in the market for Enid Blyton books, any more than the producer of other products, e.g. toothpaste, has a monopoly by being the only supplier of its brand.

Nor are the limits specified for the licensed exercise of a copyright, by reference to period, type or territory, 'restrictive practices'. The licence merely sets out the scope of a positive placement of a product on the market which otherwise, without that definition, could only be licensed in its entirety, permitting only the one licensing of the product, not an innovative range.

3. The scope of copyright

Copyright now extends to cover the following types of creative works:

- Text: authors' rights in their original writing (which may be fiction, non-fiction or e.g educational, academic, scientific writing) reproduced in books, periodicals, newspapers, letters, documents, electronic formats and other publications, together with i) publishers' rights in published editions and ii) database makers' rights in databases, reinforced by a separate *database right*.

- Music: composers' and songwriters' rights in a musical work, performance rights, recording rights, rights in a recording, and performers' rights.

- Graphics, pictures, designs and games: artists', photographers', designers' and producers' rights.

- Broadcasting, film and video: Producers' rights in a broadcast film or video, directors' rights, performers' rights.

- Software: producers' and writers' rights

In general, the author or actual creator, including of a work made for hire, is the first copyright owner, but rights to works made in the course of employment are owned by the employer.

Duration of copyright

The initial creator's right within the EU is for the life of the creator plus 70 years. This relatively long term is designed to enable a work which does not originally find a significant market (e.g. new forms of musical composition or painting) to enjoy protection at a later time when it achieves recognition, or is republished, and to give creative workers an estate which can be of value to their inheritors. Other rights (for example the producer's rights in a published edition or recording) are of shorter duration, usually commencing from the date of publication.

A new right has recently been introduced by the EU to enable artists who have sold their pictures to claim a share of the increased value of their paintings in subsequent sale, when, e.g. the artist has become famous: *droit de suite*. The UK has opted out of this right on the grounds that it might damage the international competitiveness of UK salesrooms.

International system

Internationally, the copyright system is enforced through the Berne Convention for the Protection of Literary and Artistic Works (the 'International Copyright Convention' or ICC), administered by the UN World Intellectual Property Organisation (WIPO), of which most sovereign states are signatories, supported by the Universal Copyright Convention, administered by UNESCO, which incorporates special provisions for developing countries, now also included in the ICC. Other international conventions enforce protection for other forms of copyright and works. These conventions typically establish minimum standards of protection to be accorded by signatory states to works emanating from other sovereign states, and require states to accord the same protection to foreign works as they accord to their own nationals.

More recently, to combat the growing threat of copyright piracy (commercial exploitation without the licence of the copyright owner) the World Trade Organisation established an agreement to strengthen international sanctions against piracy and to encourage greater protection of intellectual property generally, a treaty entitled *Trade Related aspects of International Property Rights* (TRIPs).

Exceptions to copyright

Copyright law, nationally and internationally, provides for various exceptions to the right to make copies, typically designed to permit uses which are within the contemplation of the parties when a work is made available, for example 'fair dealing' (UK) or 'fair use' (USA), permitting the reproduction of small parts of a work for research (non-commercial) or private study, or for criticism, reporting or review, or limited copying for education or libraries, on strict conditions. The US 'fair use' doctrine permits more copying for educational purposes than UK 'fair dealing'. Copying for private use is not a permitted exception. The ICC provides that statutory exceptions must not infringe the 'three step test' set out in the Convention: i) the reproduction must be a 'special case'; ii) the reproduction must not conflict with a normal exploitation of the work and iii) the reproduction must not unreasonably prejudice the legitimate interests of the author.

In certain cases of multiple but small-scale copying, e.g. performance of musical recordings on radio or limited photocopying in schools and colleges, systems of *collective licensing,* subject to public regulation, and usually involving the consent (or not opting out) of the copyright owner, may apply. If operated too liberally, collective licensing can undermine the working of the competitive market, and is generally most suitable for uses involving many 'small-scale' reproductions which cannot readily be controlled by the copyright owner but which have social value, in return for payments from the user distributed by collecting societies between qualifying copyright owners. It is not a portmanteau solution to the problems of commercial digital delivery in core markets. It remains an issue as to whether use of 'orphan works' (works for which the copyright owner is unknown or cannot be traced) in certain circumstances should be controlled by a collective licensing system.

Infringements of copyright

In law, infringement of copyright (making or selling copies without legal authorisation) for commercial purposes is described as *piracy*, and is subject to criminal penalties. Infringement for non-commercial purposes is a civil tort, subject to damages, statements of account, injunctions, and, for distributors given notice that a work infringes copyright, withdrawal from distribution.

It has now become common practice to describe the vast amount of illegal copying and file-sharing facilitated by the internet as 'piracy', to emphasise the damage that this does to the legitimate property of creative workers and treating it as a moral theft. In law, however, unless it is done for commercial purposes, the illegal copying is a civil tort, not a crime, and it is wrong to describe attempts to prevent illegal copying through the courts as 'criminalising' the perpetrators (let alone 'criminalising' seven million people who, in the UK, are thought to engage in this 'piracy'). In practice, legal action against private infringers is taken to establish the principle and serve as a warning to others.

In this context, the arguments are made by those who believe that copyright should not be used to prevent such activity i) that action against illegal copying of e.g. music is a luddite denial by the producers of the optimum uses of the new technology by consumers; ii) that illegal copying is often a demonstration against excessive prices charged by producers; and iii) that systems (as provided in the Digital Economy Act) to cut frequent users off from access to the internet by termination of broadband accounts are breaches of human rights of the perpetrator or of others using the same accounts. These arguments ignore the facts that most such illegal acts of copying are made in private to avoid legitimate payment, in self-interest, so are scarcely public campaigning against producer prices, and that the human rights of creative workers to protect and earn income from their creations are surely at least as important as the human rights of illegal copiers.

European Union

The EU has established legal competence in many areas of copyright, similar to that of WIPO and UNESCO internationally, but there is no comprehensive EU copyright statute or (yet, at least) a true 'single market' in copyright works, given problems of language and legal tradition. Establishing a single market involves considerable commercial and legal difficulties.

There are however copyright directives imposing minimum common standards, in particular the Information Society Directive, but the copyright statutes of member states can still have considerable differences of approach. This makes it unacceptable that copies of works made taking advantage of lower-standards should be freely imported into member states with higher standards of protection (this is known as the application of the law of the country of destination, not that of the country of origin, itself an important source of controversy for different uses of a product).

The EU situation highlights two different copyright cultures. In the UK and Republic of Ireland, the culture is based more on facilitating commercial 'exploitation' of a work. In continental Europe, it is based more on the Roman/Napoleonic tradition, protecting the rights of the author (*droit d'auteur*). In practice, the differences have been minimised, but are demonstrated by the UK standard for attracting the protection of copyright being based on 'originality' (not copying the work of a previous author), while the continental tradition requires a display of creativity. This basically affects works such as lists or low-level directories which involve compilation rather than creative input: originality is more a question of fact, creativity more a qualitative judgement. The difference has resulted in a new right being accorded by the EU to factual databases which might or might not meet higher standards of originality or creativity: the *Database Right*, not quite copyright but similar, running parallel to copyright in databases which are creative in their form.

Market or territorial rights

Copyrights, like other intellectual property rights (patents and trademarks) can be exercised separately in different sovereign states, in accordance with local law meeting the requirements of the international conventions. This may be by licences (usually exclusive) for local production and distribution for the territory, or by importing copies made in the originating territory. These territorial rights are especially important for physical products such as books, records or video, and their digital derivatives.

There is a continuing and important legal dispute over what is known as *parallel importation* or *international exhaustion of rights*. Briefly stated, this is whether the original copyright owner who has authorised the making of copies in one territory can control the future sale of those copies into other territories (parallel importation) or has 'exhausted the right' in those copies by putting them on the market in the first place, so enabling an importer in a territory to import copies which otherwise would be an infringement of a separate exclusive licence for that territory.

The trade-related aspects of intellectual property rights (TRIPs) agreement addressed this problem of international trade but failed to resolve it.

The argument revolves around the balance between encouraging production and stockholding of e.g. books or other physical copyright products in separate sovereign states, so also supporting a local producing industry and providing opportunities for indigenous creative workers, through enforceable exclusive licences for the territory, or providing consumers with access to cheaper (and possibly earlier) products from other countries – the effects of globalisation which, however, can polarise creative output in dominant trading countries such as the USA, to the detriment of innovative local enterprise and, typically, to concentration on the most popular international works. In the case of creative works, the problem is aggravated by the ability of a producer in the larger trading country to 'run on' production at marginal cost for export markets, so selling products at an artificially low price. The economies this affords can be of value for providing products at affordable prices for poorer developing countries; it is questionable whether the short-term financial benefits to consumers in developed countries of parallel importation outweigh the alternative benefits of strong local creative industries.

The arrival of international suppliers like Amazon adds a further level of complexity. Efficient logistics enable such firms to supply a vast range of products to consumers world-wide, so combating some of the polarising effects of globalisation. But the consequences for local creators, producers and retailers – and in the longer term consumers – can be profound.

Parallel importation in the US and EU

In the US, the general provision is that the copyright owner for the US cannot prevent the re-importation of copies initially sold in the US and then exported ('grey market'), but can prevent the importation of copies made elsewhere and not licensed for the US, so protecting US producers from parallel importation by foreign producers.

Within the EU, there are additional complications arising from the 'free movement of goods' and 'restrictive practices' provisions of the European treaties, whereby if copies can be lawfully sold in one member state, they cannot be prevented from importation into another. This has profound implications for English-language products, with the competition between UK and US producers, who may be separately licensed for the English language countries (UK and Republic of Ireland), and for non-English language countries in which there is nevertheless a market for English language products (the other member states). Thus, there can be parallel importation between EU member states, but the EU prohibits the importation of copies made outside the EU and not licensed for anywhere in the EU, so rejecting the concept of *international* exhaustion of rights.

The free movement of goods provisions in the EU are only applied to physical goods, such as books or records, and not e.g. digital products or broadcasts, which are subject to different provisions. With the international embrace of the internet, it could be difficult to enforce territorial rights for digital products, though given that internet traders are able to target advertisements to potential customers based on individual profiles, they are technologically capable of determining where a given customer is located, so that it is increasingly possible to protect territorial rights even for digital products.

4. Impact of digital technology and the internet

The effectiveness of the copyright system is seriously challenged by the invention and rapid growth of digital technology, in particular by the internet as a new means of access and distribution to copyright works. Digital technology enables accurate copies to be made of digitised copyright works by a user and to be copied onto any number of other discs or computers, sometimes on a commercial scale, but including many acts of copying in private or between individuals, outside the control of the copyright owner. These copies substitute for an authorised copy and threaten the ability of the copyright owner(s) to sell or license the authorised copies.

The Internet extends this problem by facilitating access to a vast volume of digitised datafiles, enabling file sharing between different users who can use the net to obtain copies held on one computer or database to any number of others, outside the conditions of licensed copying, and by the development of browsers or search engines which can cruise the net to compile vast and comprehensive lists of topics in digitised documents on websites which can then be accessed instantaneously by a single click. The ability of copyright owners to obtain a reward for such uses of their property is limited by the practicality of systems of payment, and by the ability of the user to obtain access through alternative channels of availability, avoiding payment mechanisms.

The problem has initially been most evident for software and recorded music, but is rapidly expanding to cover films and video, books, newspapers and periodicals, and games, causing major alarm to creative workers and their producers and likely threatening the viability of systematic production of works with established content-integrity, and so the ability of creative workers to obtain the returns contemplated by the copyright system.

Numerous international, EU and national studies have been made of this problem, usually acknowledging the importance of the copyright system, but wrestling with just how to adjust the system to cope with the digital revolution. On the one hand, some argue that:

- the ability of the 'consumer' or 'user' to have greatly improved access to creative works through digital technology should not be compromised by artificial restrictions imposed by copyright on that access, and that creative workers and their producers should develop new business models that take account of the new ease of access (and, by extension, that the copyright system has become impractical anyway and should not be pursued), and that to deny this is to deny the social value of new digital technology. This view has been forcefully expressed by contributors to a recent *Guardian* symposium:

  There are a few things that are on their way out, and that includes monopolies that have outlived their usefulness, the concept of 'selling copies' as a business model, 'protecting rights' as the way of making money, and using friction to get payments. (Gerd Leonhard).

  We propose that those concerned about the viability of their current operating models should first build their understanding of how their customers prefer to use their content and services, and then redesign their monetisation accordingly. (Nick Appleyard)

  while others argue that

- the supposed alternative models contemplated have hardly been visualised let alone implemented, and seem to present equal problems of lack of effectiveness, so that the future of a sensibly ordered system of creativity is threatened, and that, while the creative industries certainly need to develop new business models appropriate for digital commerce, it requires the strong support of the authorities with an appropriate legal infrastructure to enforce new models. A view perhaps well expressed by the authors of the Google share prospectus:

Our patents, trademarks, trade secrets, copyrights and all of other intellectual property rights are important assets for us . . . any significant impairment of our intellectual property rights would harm our business or our ability to compete.

The creative industries are engaged in seeking business and licensing practices which meet the demands of the marketplace in the new digital environment but which at the same time produce a proper return on investment, including returns geared to the success of a product, so encouraging investment in new and innovative products. These business models may involve subscriptions giving rights to different levels of digital usage, trial use, payment per use (possibly accumulated through a phone or service-provider bill), or e.g. online access bundled with another purchase, such as a newspaper subscription or purchase of a book or periodical. In some cases they may be operated technically through the computer or online service requiring accompanying software: 'the answer to the machine is in the machine'. One frequently-cited proposal is for producers to develop new 'value-added' digital products, e.g. with valuable added features that cannot readily be replicated and so require potential users to access the producer's website and pay whatever is required by its 'paywalls': this may not be practicable for all types of works. These innovative new models cannot be imposed by Government or industry standard practices, but need to be tested in the market place. They need, however, to be supported by the legal infrastructure afforded by copyright that enables conditions of access to be enforced.

Libraries and agglomerators

Two special problems arise in the context of the digital market.

The first involves libraries, which traditionally have the role of holding stocks of books for consultation and lending, neither of which involve breaches of copyright *per se* (note Public Lending Right, a separate right to provide compensation for the authors of loaned books). Libraries may be:

- national libraries, or libraries of equivalent significance, which are entitled by law to claim free deposit copies of all publications, which they hold as a national archive and make available to the public at their premises. There are six such libraries in the UK and Republic of Ireland.

- Public libraries, usually provided by local authorities, and providing resources for study, reference and loan

- University, school and college libraries

- Libraries, for example research libraries, in other institutions and commercial firms

'Prescribed libraries', principally non-profit libraries in the public sector, are permitted by a copyright exception to make: i) single copies of a part of a published edition (literary, dramatic or musical), or ii) a copy of an article in a periodical, for persons satisfying the librarian that they require the article for purposes of (non-commercial) research or private study and who pay the library the costs of the copying.

Deposit libraries such as the British Library provide a sophisticated service to the research community by supplying single copies of journal articles for a fee. They do not usually use deposit copies as a source of such copies, but make copies from periodicals they have purchased.

However, in the new digital environment, in which deposit libraries are archiving electronic digital materials as well as printed copies, and are digitising out-of-copyright printed texts, the libraries wish to ensure that their digital collections are as available to researchers as their archive of printed deposit copies. Initially, the US Library of Congress accepted a protocol which sought to make electronic deposit copies of works in copyright available on similar terms to printed materials, i.e. by access at a work station located in the library building. Now, however, deposit libraries are seeking to broaden this access. For out-of-copyright, public domain, materials, this is unobjectionable. More controversially, they are seeking a simple solution to enable them to make digital copies of works in copyright for which they cannot identify or find the copyright owner, so-called *orphan works*. The Digital Economy Act attempted to make some provision for a system enabling this, but this was dropped before enactment.

At the same time, organisations such as Microsoft and Google are aggregating vast arrays of content available on websites on the internet, with i) search engines and browsers which give users instant access to the content at source, ii) making their own digital copies of vast arrays of published materials, and iii) publishing their own materials, for example maps. The search function provided by these aggregators, while directing users to information they require, causes problems for the original content providers in that, they argue, the aggregators are getting income from their sites (principally from advertising revenue) by making available information published by the content providers without providing any income for the latter.

While the aggregators accept that they cannot digitise and make available content which is in copyright without the consent of the copyright owner, aggregators such as Google wish to include out-of-print materials, in copyright, in their archives under a form of collective agreement.

At the same time, public libraries, already enabled (with the consent of publishers) through the 'People's Network' to provide access for library users to a number of digital reference works either at a PC in the library premises or, by use of a library PIN, on personal computers at home, are now beginning to lend e-readers loaded with e-books. The Digital Economy Act provides that such lending of e-books should not be an infringement of copyright, but that only e-books loaded into the e-reader on the library premises should be covered by this provision. This provision has still to be implemented.

5. Conclusion

At this time, then, we have many conflicting interests engaged in the digital market, expressing conflicting opinions and with conflicting interests on the role of copyright and the means of rewarding and stimulating the creative works so essential to the future.

In conclusion, this article seeks to set out some of the questions that arise for the effective operation of the copyright sector, for overall fairness between 'suppliers' and 'users', and for the future development either of copyright or of effective alternative systems for the new generation of digital technology. The contributions that follow address the major issues from the viewpoint of different parties engaged in the debate.

Appendix: Copyright issues for debate in the digital age

As seen above, the rapid growth of digital technology in the information society raises some major problems for the future of creativity and effective information provision, which the Stationers' Company project seeks to address. These are some of the questions which arise relevant to the current debate;

- Is enforcement of rights in copyright possible when users can access copies of copyright works from the net on their own PCs and electronic readers, share the downloads with colleagues, and access works by alternative routes, e.g. avoiding pay walls?

- If so, what is needed on the part of i) copyright holders and ii) the authorities, to support viable markets? What are appropriate penalties and sanctions against commercial piracy and private infringement?

- If not, what alternative systems can be put in place to protect and reward creative enterprise? And how should they be enforced?

- Copyright prevents the making of copies of works without the authority of the copyright owner. Is it reasonable to prevent owners of physical copies of works, e.g. deposit libraries, from making digital copies to maintain their archive and make it more accessible to researchers? If so, what restrictions should be placed on access to the digitised copies? Should copyright owners be entitled to compensation for this use?

- Similarly, is it acceptable for people who own copyright works in one format, e.g. musical recordings on disc, to reformat them for use on other media? What are the limits for such reformatting?

- Is it acceptable for compilers of digital libraries to make digital copies of works for which they cannot find the copyright owner to give the appropriate authority, and if so on what terms?

- Is there room for more collective licensing of the making of digital copies to avoid cumbersome procedures, and on what terms?

- Is it acceptable for agglomerators to digitise copies of works not available on the market (e.g. out of print) and if so on what terms? Is there room for a collective licence for such works?

- Given the variety of channels now engaged in making digital copies, e.g. copyright owners going to market, deposit libraries, public libraries, agglomerators, special agencies, retailers and distributors, each offering different terms for access, from zero to full commercial value, how can a fair market be established?

- How far is it appropriate to widen 'exceptions' to the rights of copyright holders for public service activities such as libraries and education?

- How far should it be possible to enforce territorial rights enabling separate marketing in the face of growing globalisation?

- Is the current duration of creators' copyright at 'life plus 70 years' appropriate for the digital age? Would many problems, e.g. of orphan and out-of-print works, be reduced by a shorter period, e.g. the longer of 'life' or 50 years from publication?

- Would it be practicable to aid identification of works protected by copyright through a system of public registration, as with patents and trademarks (currently forbidden by the international copyright conventions)?

Tomorrow's Humanities

JAMES MURDOCH

ADDRESS AT THE LAUNCH OF THE UCL CENTRE FOR DIGITAL
HUMANITIES , THE GUSTAVE TUCK LECTURE THEATRE,
UNIVERSITY COLLEGE LONDON, 20 MAY 2010

James Murdoch was appointed Chairman and Chief Executive, Europe and Asia, News Corporation, in 2007. In this role, he has direct responsibility for the strategic and operational development of News Corporation's television, newspaper and related digital assets in Europe, Asia and the Middle East. At the same time, James was appointed Non-Executive Chairman of BSkyB and re-joined the Board of News Corporation.

James served as BSkyB's Chief Executive Officer from November 2003 to December 2007. Prior to his appointment as CEO of BSkyB, he spent three years, from May 2000 to 2003, as Chairman and Chief Executive Officer of STAR, News Corporation's Asian satellite television and multimedia group.

Before joining STAR, James was Executive Vice President of News Corporation in New York, where he was responsible for various interactive media ventures and corporate development projects.

James serves on the Board of Yankee Global Enterprises, the Board of Trustees of the Harvard Lampoon and the Leadership Council of The Climate Group. James joined the Board of GlaxoSmithKline as a Non-Executive Director in May 2009.

Introduction

It is a great honour for me to deliver the first annual lecture of the University College London Centre for Digital Humanities. I want to use this opportunity tonight, not only to celebrate the mission of the Centre, but also to reflect with you more widely on technology, culture and society.

I'd like tonight in particular to discuss the consequences for creativity of this digital world we now live and work in. To think about the implications of universal connectivity; of the instant distribution of content; and of an imbalance that exists between the humanities and technology.

Tomorrow's Humanities

I count myself lucky to work in the creative industries, a sector populated by companies that increasingly operate across all parts of the digital world. Our business – News Corporation – is just one of those companies.

Today we publish atlases – that business at Collins is two centuries old – as well as *Wolf Hall*; we make movies and TV, from *Avatar* to *Slumdog Millionaire*, to National Geographic documentaries and *Glee*; we publish *The Sun* every day; more Bibles than anyone else in the world; and the world's pre-eminent business newspaper, *The Wall Street Journal*.

That breadth prompts some thoughts which I would like to share with you, whether you are a scholar, an engineer, or an artist. Whatever your background and viewpoint.

I make these remarks at a time of great debate about the future of journalism. Many voices predict its demise as it goes through a transition from being a medium that is predominantly physical to one that is predominantly digital. It is in this context of real consequence that *The Times* and *The Sunday Times* will soon become among the first papers in the world to assert a fair value for their online editions.

I am particularly delighted to be here tonight because the mission of the Centre is something that is important to me. There is some irony in a college drop-out addressing such a distinguished audience, in such a distinguished place. An early flirtation with Academia, starting as a teenage volunteer with a pick axe – more hard labour than ivory tower, I learned – and ending some years later in the bowels of the British School at Rome, was never going to get me here.

My career has since taken a somewhat different path. But it has remained, I would say, absolutely within the same field: because today's creative industries are tomorrow's humanities.

As a discipline, the digital humanities have grown from the simple use of databases in scholarly work, to an approach championed here at UCL: a partnership in which technology is neither the servant of the humanities, nor its master, but an equal partner. The result has been a balance that has fostered innovation on both sides.

To take one example from the work you do here: the digital exploration of the complex stratigraphy of the Vindolanda tablets from Hadrian's Wall. That work has led in turn to the improvement of scanning and diagnosis of breast cancer.

Or how 3D imaging is being improved through the challenge of being applied to ancient material like the fragments of the Thera frescoes: tiny pieces of which can now be recombined more accurately and quickly than could have been achieved by human eye and hand.

And I must also mention the project that aims to bring together the voluminous unpublished writings of Jeremy Bentham into a single digital resource. This is an act both of scholarship, and of filial piety towards one of the founding fathers of University College itself. And I understand that Bentham himself will be presiding – both in spirit and in body – over our drinks later tonight.

These initiatives – and there are many more – reflect the way in which the world of scholarship now has the benefit of technology that would have amazed a scholar working even a decade ago, let alone in Bentham's day.

Italo Calvino memorably put the reader in a network of lines that intersect in his groundbreaking mystery of misprints, lost endings, found beginnings, and unexpected ordering out of chaos – *If on a Winter's Night a Traveller*. We find ourselves at such a nexus today. We have little regard to geography, or indeed time: we are always in a centre of learning, at an intersection of opportunities. We can study NASA's photographs of exploding galaxies, Darwin's papers, or Lincoln's letters, with ease. We can jump from one place – the Sky News app – to another – the shopping basket waiting to be delivered – all on our smart-phones, at the tap of a finger.

It brings to mind Bilbo Baggins' half-warning, half-dare to his second cousin: "It's a dangerous business … going out of your door…you step onto the Road, and if you don't keep your feet, there is no knowing where you might be swept off to."

That road is open to us all the time, wherever and whoever we are. We are immersed in a digital world, at an intersection of infinite possibility and complexity. This is not some sort of prediction. The boundaries between types of media have already gone. Every one of our cultural and creative activities can be expressed as a series of ones and zeros. And because they have a common environment, you can flow them into one another and mix them up, virtually without friction, or any sense of physical time and space.

Tonight I want to ask what that world means for the balance between technology and creativity. To ask whether that balance has been upset. Whether the relationship between creators and their rights, and the means of distribution, needs to be reformed.

I want also to try to put into context the prevailing consensus about the digital world and the way in which it works – the consensus that the free flow of information not only can, but must, literally, be free.

I want to inquire – as dispassionately and factually as I can – into what drives that consensus ... because I believe that the digital consensus is flawed. Although expressed in terms of high principle and morality, it is more revealing to study the economics of the thing – to find out what's really going on.

I want to show you that restoring the balance between creators and the means of distribution would be a huge spur to creative growth ... and that an approach based on experience – on a proven approach to protecting creative vision – is the key to a thriving creative sector and a rich and continuing tradition of these digital humanities.

Is digital world straightforwardly utopian?

Forgive me if I sound foreboding. I know – the established consensus about the digital world today is straightforwardly utopian.

First, it has a firm belief that the old rules relating to physical things like books and music are simply irrelevant to the digital world, so there is no point in looking back. As many people put it, we have a new paradigm: we all own everything, so no-one owns anything. The internet – and everything on it, it is said – wants to be free.

Second, digital networks are depicted as forces of nature. The idea that anyone might try to shape the future, to influence events, to innovate with an outcome, is seen as foolish – or indeed out-of-touch.

You can see why this vision appeals. It feels radical and new. It makes sense of some of the things that we see around us. And a lot of digital change is genuinely exciting and fun to be involved in. Anyone who has watched the two minute and 18 second retelling of the entire Star Wars trilogy – in Lego – will know what I mean.

Yet there are some immediate concerns. We cannot just assume that greater connectivity is a force for good in and of itself.

It might be easy to assert that if everyone, everywhere, can access anything with a browser and a broadband connection, then our society – all societies – are going to be wiser, better-informed and more democratic. In many ways that is true. But we must not be naïve to the fact that this frictionless society is one which is uncharted – and human behaviour in a context of ultimate plurality – huge choice and connected everywhere – is still a new subject.

We certainly have easier, faster, cheaper ways to share with each other. But we have to face the fact that a huge amount of the capacity now available is used to distribute things without the permission of their creators, let alone any payment to them. In the first quarter of this year alone, there were 190 million downloads of Hollywood content in just 20 countries. You can add to that substantial illegal web streaming, where viewers watch without downloading. This is not the stuff of a few students outwitting the system. It is deliberate and on an industrial scale.

The numbers continue to show that well over half of all internet traffic consists of illegal file sharing and other forms of piracy.

I am struck by the number of commentators who switch seamlessly from one strongly moral argument in favour of free content as being good for society: to another which seems to me to be completely immoral: saying that we can't stop people distributing content without permission, so we may as well give everyone the right to do so.

Finally, it is true that new models of ownership and commercial activity have developed in the networked world. And, indeed, that many people like to share their material for nothing greater than the simple recognition of their authorship. But is it right to assume that the system will only allow for everyone's doing so? All of the time?

Who gains?

Now would be a good time to pause, and to ask: who gains? Why are these utopian arguments so prevalent and powerful? In whose interest is their primacy?

Putting the rhetoric of freedom to one side, what we can see is a number of competing interests on a common digital terrain.

Let's start with creative companies – and remember I work for one. Although they range in size from global players to one-man shops, every one of them has a clear interest in producing creative material that people want to buy – for a fair price. They have an interest in ensuring that creators are incentivised to continue to produce material that audiences want. They naturally place a high value on independent creativity.

Other companies have completely different incentives. Take the search business. It depends on an ability to index and search other people's material, and present the results of those searches to its users surrounded by advertising. Search is a highly profitable business, because the raw material presented to customers can be indexed at essentially zero incremental cost. Therefore, information that might only be searched or indexed with a fair price paid to the producer undermines that model.

What is often absent from the public's understanding and commentators' calculation, is that without investment in original content in the first place, there will be little to index, search, and aggregate.

We should also consider consumer electronics companies and device makers. Devices – however smart they look and however innovative they are – are lifeless without content. Manufacturers have a clear incentive to drive the cost of content toward zero – in order to drive customers to buy their products, without additional competition from rights-holders for their customers' money.

This digital terrain is crowded – but it's not only populated by commercial interests.

A public body like the British Library, for example, is not driven by a bottom line. But as an organisation, the Library has a clear incentive to extend the range of its services as widely as possible and thus secure more public funding to do so.

This is a circular process: funding drives new activity, which creates more requests for funding; popularity makes demands on the public purse easier to bear. Take the current controversy over the Library's intention to provide unrestricted access to digital material. Material that publishers originally produced – and continue to make available – for commercial reasons. Like the search business, but motivated by different concerns, the public sector interest is to distribute content for near zero cost – harming the market in so doing, and then justifying increased subsidies to make up for the damage it has inflicted.

The case of the British Library goes even further. Just yesterday, the Library announced the digitisation of their newspaper archive – originally given to them by publishers as a matter of legal obligation. This is not simply being done for posterity, nor to make free access for library users easier, but also for commercial gain via a paid-for website. The move is strongly opposed by major publishers. If it goes ahead, free content would not only be a justification for more funding, but actually become a source of funds for a public body.

When we look over this terrain, we can see the economic pressures driving down the value of content are very powerful. Arguments over rights and wrongs seem little more than a disguise for self-interest.

'So what?' you might say. That's competition. And in large part I would agree with you. But I would urge you to bear two things in mind.

Cultural content has a social importance

First, cultural content has a social importance different from, say, the automobile or energy markets, and beyond its economic contribution – because it is the sphere of ideas, imagination, accountability and communication. Its economic – and therefore self-perpetuating – independence is essential to the functioning of a democratic society.

If you want to understand why that matters, look at journalism.

Journalism was the making of News Corporation; it is still fundamental to what we do; and we believe utterly and completely in the contribution independent journalism makes to a free society.

Journalism – print and digital – faces trouble

Yet journalism – print and digital – faces trouble. In the last year in the U.S. alone, 109 newspapers shut down or stopped publishing a print edition, leaving many cities without a single paper.

The reasons are not hard to understand. Search companies and aggregators skim content from a thousand sources, sell it to clients, scoop up advertising revenues and put little or nothing back into professional newsgathering.

Second, many of the pressures on content – journalism included – are caused by governments. Frankly, states provide a level of subsidised news that is: incredibly high; comprehensive; and well funded.

The creative industries are not without blame – acquiescing, or simply not reacting, for far too long. But that period is ending.

I believe that if there is an imbalance between the providers of creativity and those who exploit it, then we should care about it, and do something about it. Not in the interests of a particular company or sector. It is the public whose interest we need to serve – both people now, and future generations who deserve to enjoy the richness and diversity of material that we know we are capable of producing.

My questions this evening are therefore simple but fundamental.

What should we do to restore balance to the system?

Do we at present have a fair balance? I do not believe we have, and I fear that the problem is growing rapidly worse. Has it moved against the creators in favour of distributors, whether public or private? In my view, yes it has: and it has done so decisively.

What should we do to restore balance to the system? Is there anything that we can do? The answer is simpler than you might think.

An Act for the Encouragement of Learning

On the wall behind me you see the words: 'Remember the days of old: consider the years of each generation'. Of all places, in this room we should be mindful of that maxim in answering those questions. Because we have been here before as a society, and we have arrived at rather different conclusions to those of the digital consensus that I described a moment ago.

We happen to be almost exactly at the three-hundredth anniversary of one of the first codifications of intellectual property rights: the introduction of literary copyright into British law. In 1710 – on the 10 April, to be exact – Parliament passed the so-called Statute of Anne. I'll quote from its preamble, in which it announces itself to be:

> *An Act for the Encouragement of Learning, by Vesting the Copies of Printed Books in the Authors or Purchasers of such Copies, during the Times therein mentioned.*

It then explains what had been happening:

> *Whereas Printers, Booksellers, and other Persons, have of late frequently taken the Liberty of Printing, Reprinting, and Publishing, or causing to be Printed, Reprinted, and Published Books, and other Writings, without the Consent of the Authors or Proprietors of such Books and Writings, to their very great Detriment, and too often to the Ruin of them and their Families…*

And it goes on to say that a law should be enacted:

...For Preventing therefore such Practices for the future, and for the Encouragement of Learned Men to Compose and Write useful Books.

The Statute was a reaction to a time of unprecedented techno-logical change. Printing presses offered the prospect of cheap copies of books, and the knowledge they contained, for the many instead of just the elite. Low-cost copying and distribution had created a revo-lution in access to information.

The approach of the authorities in Britain to the invention of printing, as in most countries, had at first been control and censor-ship. For many years in English law there had been a legal cartel in printing: only members of the Stationers' Company were permitted to publish books.

In 1695 the Stationer's monopoly was allowed to lapse, and when it was finally replaced fifteen years later, the Statute of Anne ushered in a transformative new approach.

Not only did the Statute create for the first time in English law a system of copyright, but crucially it recognised also the rights of the author – the creator – alongside that of the printer and bookseller.

The legislature had listened to the voices of those, like John Locke and Daniel Defoe, who had argued that – and I quote: 'To print another Man's copy is much worse than robbing him on the Highway; for the Thief takes only what he finds about him, but the Pyrate Printer takes away his inheritance ... [which] both is and ought to be the Due, not of the Author only, but of his Family and Children.'

The Statute was the start of the development of a system of copy-right and of authors' rights that now extends to forms of creativity that were undreamt of in the days of Queen Anne, and to issues way beyond the regulation of the London book trade.

The statute reflected and encouraged the transition in literature from a system in which aristocratic patronage was key – a state of affairs that had existed since at least the time of Augustus and Vergil – to that in which writing became a profession at which one could make a living. This was the era of Pope, and Johnson, and writers after them.

It is not a coincidence that Pope himself was a keen litigant in matters affecting his intellectual property, or that Johnson's most famous remark is directly concerned with the economics of creativity. 'No man but a blockhead ever wrote, except for money' has become worn by over-use, and was in part a joke: but it carries a clear message about the reality and opportunity of late 18th Century literary life.

Of course, wealthy people still today commission art works or make gifts to museums. Patronage is far from dead. But copyright developed a way to provide the creator with an income into the future: a longer term in which more creation was enabled, and authors could control their careers and pursue their visions.

If you want a neat example of this then consider Dickens, many of whose novels were published chapter by chapter with a popularity directly reflected in the sale of weekly or monthly magazines – a creative discipline which anyone who has worked in commercial television, particularly in the United States, will immediately recognise.

The Statute of Anne was an attempt to control piracy and balance the interests of authors, printers and the reading public – a balance beneficial to all.

By the standards of today's digital consensus the Statute would have to be regarded as a colossal mistake. Instead, we should surely applaud the wisdom and foresight of the legislators of three hundred years ago.

They looked to the long-term interests of society and the creative industries of their time. Their innovation helped to usher in a period of growth in publishing, writing and journalism, and in the size of the reading public.

The recognition by the Statute of Anne of the rights of authors was primarily an economic one. But I do not need to convince this audience that author's rights mean far more than simply providing for a financial return for the creator.

Today, copyright gives creators the right to be credited for their work. The vast majority of things are not written for money, at least not directly, despite Dr Johnson's jest: the American Declaration of Independence; the wartime speeches of Winston Churchill; or the outpourings of innumerable bloggers are not the creatures of royalty payments. But nor are they thrown aside by their authors. Attribution and the ability to prevent plagiarism are just as important to most writers as commercial return, as the legion of creators licensing their work under the Creative Commons attests.Copyright also can be transferred to others, for the benefit of society, as the Great Ormond Street hospital enjoys royalties on Barrie's Peter Pan; as does Westminster School for the works of A. A. Milne.

This is not a zero-sum game. If you want to offer your product for free, then there is nothing to stop you – and it's a lot easier these days to do so. The only temptation you need to resist is the idea that what you want to do is what everyone else should be made to do.

The defining characteristic of the world created by the Statute of Anne and its successors has been the protection it offers to artists: and the encouragement that it provides to risk.

It opens up a literally boundless world for a determined individual with a creative vision. A good example is James Cameron, the film director. As someone who cares very deeply about the environment, he had been thinking for well over a decade about making a film around the impact of reckless human exploitation of natural resources. A film that would transfer the action to another, delicately realised and completely self-consistent world.

To do that properly required two things: massive advances in computational power – rendering a whole new world is no simple math problem; and a partner with the willingness to risk huge sums on a belief that the story would resonate with people across the world.

The result – as I am sure you will have guessed by now – was the movie *Avatar*. There are not many companies willing to risk a quarter of a billion dollars on a single project – but ours was one of them. We believed in Jim Cameron and we knew that technology was ready to transform the way we can create and tell stories in audio-visual media.

Nor was *Avatar* innovative in a merely technical sense. Cameron's attention to detail extended to a whole new language, the Na'vi tongue. At long last those with a master's degree in Orcish now have a fresh challenge.

In the process, the investment in *Avatar* gave us major advances in the 3D technology that looks likely to be the next mainstream innovation in both movies and television. A technology now being applied to other worlds – literally – as Jim has shown interest in improving the visual capability of the next NASA Mars Explorer.

But *Avatar* is not typical. The importance of 3D was not just that it made the film so exciting to watch: it also made it relatively less attractive to copy and view illegally. Other films now have their profits routinely looted through piracy.

The workprint of one film, *Wolverine*, was stolen and posted on the internet and then downloaded 14 million times prior to theatrical release. It has now been downloaded more than 25 million times – with five European countries accounting for much of the total. This shows that great damage can be done at lightning speed.

We might seem to have come a long way from the work of a few gentlemen debating the rights of booksellers and authors in 1710. But we have not.

The principles set out in the Statute of Anne represented a major step forward in the free flow of ideas.

It recognised that piracy would have led to a long-term decline in the distribution of books.

It provided for a system in which creativity was incentivised – an engine for the development of knowledge and learning – just at a time when a fully literate society was beginning to emerge.

Three hundred years later, and after innumerable books, plays, movies, TV shows, and assorted flotsam, jetsam, and lagan, we can say that the champions of the Statute of Anne offer us lessons we should continue to learn from and apply.

We need to approach the future of the creative industries

In conclusion, I believe that we need to approach the future of the creative industries – the future of the humanities in other words – in an economically serious way – as we should do with all forms of enterprise.

This is a significant sector. In 2008 it represented some 7% of the total wealth created annually in the European Union – some €860 billion – and provided some 14 million people with jobs. Yet billions annually are lost to piracy and a cumulative total not far short of 200,000 jobs have already gone.

That suggests that we should recognise the fundamental role that property rights play in the making of cultural things. Compared to the exciting rhetoric of the need for everything to be free, that might seem unglamorous, unromantic, and indeed hard-hearted. But it may be all of those things and yet still be a better road for our society to take.

Do not be misled by claims of high principle in this debate. When someone tells you content wants to be free, what you should hear is 'I want your content for free ' – and that is not the same thing at all.

We must rediscover something that should be very obvious: the importance of placing a proper value on creative endeavour.

Just look at the newspaper business. For years, many newspapers have put no value at all on the work they place online. In contrast, at News International here in the UK, we are proud of the quality of our journalism and the contribution we make to life around the country, and indeed for our readers around the world.

We are one of the largest employers of journalists and editors, and maintain an incomparable range of foreign correspondents, contributors and bureaux in all sorts of places. We attach a fair value and a fair price to the journalism we produce. What is so controversial about that?

Shouldn't we welcome a revolution in journalism that answers the needs of readers – and provides the means for sustained further investment? Without some simple common sense – like this – the alternative we face is a grim one: to have news that is produced only by the wealthy, the amateur, or the government.

Asserting a fair value for digital journalism is a starting point. I don't think we will be alone in taking this kind of action. And although these steps have provoked some alarmist comment, no-one who really cares about the humanities of tomorrow should be either shocked or affronted by what we are doing.

Can we agree that preserving and rewarding creativity is in the long-term interest of our society?

This problem will not be solved by the creative sector alone. Governments should enforce basic property rights – even in this digital environment. Some have started. In some quarters this has caused alarm. But what is really alarming is that it is controversial at all to shut down vast pirate sites or disconnect repeat offenders who have no regard for creators' rights.

According to a detailed study by Tera Consultants, if we continue down the path we're on, piracy could inflict a cumulative 1.2 million job losses in the European Union by 2015.

Is it, moreover, unreasonable to suggest that companies that make a living out of indexing and sharing the creativity of others might make a fair contribution to those who create the material they need for their businesses?

Should it be controversial to suggest that public bodies are prevented from endlessly extending their remits, profiting from work they do not create, or dampening innovation and investment?

Three hundred years ago, when statesmen wrestled with these issues, they struck a fair balance between the rights of creators and the power of technology. We must do the same:

- Creative industries must develop and protect the value of what they create;

- Public bodies should be restrained from crowding out productive investment;

- Government should act to ensure that the copyright framework in this 21st century digital environment is fully functional; to stimulate future growth and diversity of creativity, by respecting and reaffirming these basic rights.

By taking action and showing commitment, we can succeed in addressing the imbalance that exists today. We can change things for the better, as society has done before at times of technological change.

In this success, when the statute of Anne has its four hundredth birthday – and this Centre marks its centenary – there will be a whole new set of things to study and whole new eras of human output to celebrate.

We shall still then be able to say that human society, culture and creativity is growing ever richer.

Do Libraries Dream of Electric Sheep?

LISBET RAUSING

Lisbet Rausing is a Senior Research Fellow at Imperial College's Centre for the History of Science, Technology and Medicine.

She was educated at the University of California Berkeley and Harvard University, where she also taught for eight years. She has written two academic monographs as well as numerous scholarly articles.

Together with her husband, Peter Baldwin, Lisbet Rausing founded Arcadia in 2001. Arcadia protects endangered treasures of culture and nature. This includes near extinct languages, rare historical archives and museum quality artefacts, as well as threatened landscapes. Partners include Harvard, Yale, SOAS, the British Library, the Ashmolean, the Linnean Society, Imperial College, Cambridge University, Oxford University and Fauna & Flora International. More information can be found at www.arcadiafund. org.uk.

Lisbet Rausing chairs Nyland, a Rausing family office, which together with other entities supports her family and its wealth management, and works with operational family companies such as Ecolean, a liquid food packaging company, and Ingleby, a global farming company. She serves on various boards and committees including the Harvard Board of Overseers, and Yad Hanadiv.

She holds honorary doctorates from Uppsala University, Imperial College and SOAS, is an elected member of St Catherine's College, Cambridge. She is an Honorary Fellow of the British Academy, a Fellow of the Linnean Society and the Royal Historical Society.

Abstract: Imagine a New Alexandria. Imagine a library that contains the natural and social sciences of the West, peer-reviewed publications, archives, and collections. It is electronic and in the public domain: stable, linked and searchable. New Alexandria demands an ethos of digital conservation, scholarship and public access. It needs to be a long-term public good, hosted by reputable non-profit institutions, in stable jurisdictions. But it is technically possible.

After all, Google Books aims for c. 16 million books,[1] and the non-profit Internet Archive has c. 1 million volumes.

We live in the age of electronic reproduction. The technological future is certain, and it is created by scholars, entrepreneurs and amateurs, in a Schumpeterian process of creative destruction. Even our most traditional products of learning (monographs, academic articles, etc.) are dis-intermediating. As marginal costs of replicas near zero, what constitutes an archive, a publisher, a bookseller, or a book, is all put in question. Things fly apart at the seams.

The question is not whether change is coming. It is who will be the change-makers. This is not a challenge of technology or finances. It is not, even, a question of law, though copyright legislation is fiendishly destructive of the democratisation of scholarly knowledge. This challenges state-builders and gatekeepers: academics, librarians, foundation staff, politicians and civil servants. Can we build structures that will preserve and order, but also share and disseminate, the world's learning and cultures? It is a challenge of will and imagination. Here, I discuss three such challenges: the cult of the artefact, the problem of abundance, and the question of the audience.

Do Libraries Dream of Electric Sheep?[2]

The cult of the artefact is a story of our imaginary horizons. Our iconic library stories are romances of destruction, decay and amnesia. We still mourn Alexandria. We revere St Catherine's Monastery, the Vatican archives, and the Dead Sea Scrolls. We grieve over the Christians closing the academy of Athens, and over the fall of Constantinople, where in desperation the last Grecian scholars lit the cannons with their manuscripts. Boethius, the monks of Iona, the fleeing Byzantine humanists – these are our heroes and role models.

---

[1] Harvard has nearly 16 million items but about half of those are periodicals. About 7 million are books, and of those, three-quarters come from outside the US, although serious collecting abroad only started from the 1860s.

[2] I derive the title from Philip K Dick's futuristic novel *Do Androids Dream of Electric Sheep* (New York: Doubleday, 1968), which also formed the basis of the 1982 film *Blade Runner*.

Perhaps this is why the great libraries of the West concern themselves so centrally with the single and exceptional object, while hiding the purchases of scholarly databases in their yearly reports' sub-clauses and footnotes. But should we rejoice when dwindling acquisition budgets are spent on "rare books," "rare," admittedly, but not in a meaningful sense threatened or endangered? And if so, why? Throughout history, libraries have struggled against destruction. They still operate within an imaginary economy of scarcity – attempting to "save" rare books. But what does that code of "rescue" denote, except a Benjaminian cult of the physical artefact?

In an era of electronic abundance, how can libraries archive the dreams and experiences of humankind? What do we discard? If a library is no longer a warehouse of treasures, what is it? Harvard's c. 16 million volumes rival those of Google Books. One collection took nearly four-hundred years to achieve: the other, less than a decade. Harvard's ambitions in 1638 were universal: to hold all knowledge. But how can this be achieved today?

Bibliographies, dictionaries, encyclopaedias, library catalogues, scholarly journals and so on are all dematerializing, as they move into "the cloud."[3] But what about processes rather than products of knowledge, such as lab books, lectures, conference proceedings, data sets, and course work? The papers of Newton, Darwin, Einstein, and Bohr were finite. But what about "big science"? The Large Hadron Collider at CERN takes 90 million measurements 600 million times a second, analysed by c. 6,000 physicists. How is that to be archived? Worldwide, scientific data files are approaching a pet-

---

[3] "The cloud," a dematerialized and outsourced network, consists of huge data centres with software applications used by millions of people at the same time. Yahoo, Wikipedia, YouTube, Twitter, Amazon, and so on are all built on such centres. Indeed, Amazon is transforming itself from a book seller to a cloud-space renter, in Amazon Web Services, which already uses more bandwidth than its retail side. Its Simple Storage Service has c. 52 billion virtual objects. In manufacturing, a parallel to "the cloud" might be "outsourcing". A more homely example might be how your music experience moves from CDs, to JPEGs on your hard drive, to Pandora, which is situated in a cloud. Feature length films are of course next. What household would not appreciate instantaneous rental films from "the long tail" (the entire backlist) of Hollywood, or for that matter all the other film industries of the world? *Herald Tribune*, 15 June 2009.

abyte.[4] Every year, they double. Even artisanal lab skills are now recorded, on wikis.[5]

Our Alexandria was not burnt, our Byzantium still stands, and our Athenian academies are blossoming. And next to our scholarly endeavours, and our rare, well-studied, cultic artefacts, we want to preserve ephemera—esoteric traditions, dying languages, oral memories. We now know that we understand only slowly what will last through the ages. What if our next "peasant poet," as John Clare was known, twitters,[6] writes a blog or shojo manga, or publishes via a desktop? Is that legal deposit? What if a Nigerian novelette (typically addressing a young heroine's agonized choice between a village boy and a "big man") is written by a Jane Austen?

If we record / remember everything, then what will a library (selective, ordered) look like.

What is the library when we can safeguard memory and images themselves and complete: if we record / remember everything, then what will a library (selective, ordered) look like? What happens when people think the "canon" means an online strategy war game, or a shojo manga? What is the library in the era of the internet (1974), the web (1991), or Google (1998)? What is the library in its Second Life?[7]

In 2008, Tim Berners-Lee noted that the web can be modelled by biological concepts: plasticity, population dynamics, food chains,

---

[4]   10 to the fifteenth power, or quadrillion.

[5]   Take for example the 2005 wiki OpenWetWare, started by biological engineers at MIT, which unexpectedly morphed into a vast manual of lab techniques, alongside its original function as a collection of laboratory notebooks. Mitchell Waldrop, "Science 2.0," *Scientific American,* May 2008, p. 47-51.

[6]   Presently, Google worries about how their Twitter searches are indexed when they are a few minutes old, rather than in real time. Herald Tribune, 15 June 2009.

[7]   Second Life refers to an online virtual world where scientists have begun conducting real research projects, essentially on Darwinist theory, while taking on digital alter egos. It was founded in 2003 by Linden Lab as an open-ended platform where users (avatars) can create their own environment. It is, if you will, an open-ended SIM world, and it had c 13.5 million users in mid-2008. By that date, its SciLands had grown into a mini-continent of some 45 islands – of, admittedly, nearly a thousand in all – inhabited not only by individual scientists but also by more of 300 universities and museums as well as by organisations such as NASA. Science News, 24 May 2008, pp. 20-23.

and ecosystems.[8] Does understanding the web mean grasping its quasi-biological whole? Do libraries dream of electric sheep? Do electric sheep dream of libraries? Will Second Life take on life? And if so, what will be its – and our – library?

¤ ¤ ¤ ¤

As the open web movement has it, an old tradition and a new technology together enable an unprecedented public good.[9] The "new technology" means that the near-zero marginal costs of electronic replicas allows disintermediation. The "old tradition" means that scholars publish without pay, for peer recognition and social utility. Universities, recognizing this, say they "produce, preserve, and propagate knowledge." But look closely at their libraries. They serve their faculty and students, and, when feasible, scholars at peer institutions. They do not serve the public.

Fifty years ago, that may not have mattered. But today, people are educated and engaged. As disinterested scholars, they participate in the collective projects of knowledge the technological rupture has enabled, such as Wikipedia, GalaxyZoo, ESP, Africa@home, Herbaria@home or SETI.[10] This mass voluntary participation at times is "grunt work," related to image recognition.[11] But scholars also engage with the "hive mind," or the public, in complex or interpretative work. For example, the Rothschild family and others are putting the Dead Sea Scroll fragments into the public domain, engaging with religious communities that have unparalleled language skills.

---

[8] Nigel Shadbolt and Tim Berners-Lee, "Web Science Emerges," *Scientific American*, October 2008.

[9] Freedom for IP, "Budapest Open Access Initiative," 19 November 2007: http://freedomforip.org/category/open-access/.

[10] SETI (the Search for Extra Terrestrial Intelligence) has three million people donating spare computer time to seek for narrow bandwidth radio signals in space. In Folding@home, some 40,000 PlayStation 3 volunteers help Stanford scientists fold proteins. In foldReCAPTCHA, amateurs digitise the *New York-Times's* back catalogue. In the ESP project, the public has labelled c. 50 million photographs (to help computers think). In GalaxyZoo, c. 160,000 people help John Hopkins astronomers to classify galaxies, and in Africa@home, volunteers help the University of Geneva create Africa maps through satellite images. Conservation biology depends on amateur surveys, and at Herbaria@home, volunteers decipher herbaria in British museums.

[11] Crowdsourcing is also of course a tool for political activists. It is used to demonstrate corruption (by tracing the flights of Tunisia's presidential jet), to find war criminals (in Darfur), or to advocate changes in the Catholic Church. *The Economist Technology Quarterly*, 6 September 2008, 8-10.

But on the whole, scholars exclude the public from their "core" research materials, such as House of Commons Parliamentary Papers, Historical Statistics of the United States Online, BMJ Clinical Evidence, Early English Literature Online, ehRAF Collection of Ethnography, Index of Christian Art, Index Islamicus, Oxford Music Online, and ARTstor. Many commercially owned databases demand eye-watering fees, and / or only allow institutional subscribers. Even university-controlled collections are expensive.

It is a scandal that academic databases and research tools are unavailable to the public. After all, the public has paid for them – through research grants, tax breaks, and donations. Why should only scholars affiliated to universities have access to PhDs, MAs, and JSTOR?[12]

Academic databases are at least digital. Public access—the right to roam–is a press-of-the-button away. But academic monographs, while produced digitally, are then – in an act of collective academic madness – turned into non-searchable paper. And all academic writing, digital or not, is kept from the public domain for the authors' lifetime plus seventy years.

Academic materials, being a public good, should obviously not fall under commercial copyright. Nor should "orphan" works (out-of-print books, without known copyright holders). But restrictive fair use rules mean that libraries do not dare digitalize their orphan works. In the age of electronic reproduction, many books remain as rare as Gutenberg Bibles.

Today, scholars – working for public institutions, paid by tax payers – sign over their copyright to for-profit presses and journals. At best, they illicitly put their research on their websites. A "don't ask don't tell" stand-off means that free public access to scholarship exists only in fragments, in violation of copyright, and by means of unstable self-archiving.

To copyright legislation, add market failure. The inflation rate for scholarly monographs is high, and prices are hyper-inflating for commercial academic journals, where three firms control over 80% of the market. The price per page for commercial journals is up to 12 times more than for non-profit ones, and not because they are better. In the field of economics, the cost per citation is 16 times higher in

---

[12] JSTOR is said to have hundreds of millions of referrals from Google a year, the vast majority of which are refusals. There is considerable internet rage over JSTOR being closed.

commercial journals than those published by scholarly societies.[13] More recently, Google and the publishing industry have created "an effective cartel," with "significant barriers to entry." As the FT rightly has noted, an "effective monopoly provider" always eventually charges monopolistic and discriminatory prices: "just as happened with academic journals in the past."[14]

Let's rehearse once more how university research is disseminated today: publicly funded institutions first give away, and then buy back, their own research. Adding insult to injury, the scholars who sign over their copyrights for free to for-profit journals, also donate their labour for free, as volunteer peer reviewer and editors. It is, shall we say, an unusual business model: the producer gives away a product he then buys it back, having helped the intermediary package it.

There are worthwhile initiatives to make scholarship public. Some 10% of Anglophone academic journals are now open access. The "gold" ones are edited and peer-reviewed, and with prestige-factors equalised, citation rates are significantly higher from open access articles.[15] Yet as long as journals and university press brands are a proxy for quality to tenure committees, the stranglehold of commerce will remain. This stranglehold is not only ravaging university budgets. It also blocks the emergence of a wise and learned commonwealth, by disallowing free access to good, peer-reviewed data. Arguably, this is also a legal, freedom of information matter.

We thus urgently need better laws and wiser funding of university research. Our nudges need to go the other way. Why not presume open access, along the lines of presuming organ donor intent? Why not make copyright something that needs to be asserted and renewed? Could copyright automatically lapse, when it stops generating income? Should not university presses release their tax-financed backlists into the public domain? Could university libraries make alumni members? Should university library catalogues be

---

[13] "Improving Scholarly Publishing Practice at Harvard: Report on the Provost's Committee on Scholarly Publishing," Harvard, p 5. The report notes that commercial publisher's profits for scholarly journals are estimated at around 40%, an astonishingly high figure for any industry.

[14] *Financial Times* (London edition), 19 June 2009.

[15] A now-classic *Nature* article of 2001, "Online or invisible?" (Vol 411, nr 6837) analysed c 120,000 articles in computer science from 1989 to 2000. It found that, standardized for age-cohort, public domain articles had 4.5 times more citations. The correlation also held for top-end articles, from prestigious conferences.

turned into blogs, allowing university members – or the public – to add commentaries and hyperlinks?

Institutions need to take a stance. Think only of the British Library's feeble response to the 2006 Gowers Review of Intellectual Property: it pleaded for unpublished works to have "only" a copyright of life plus 70 years,[16] and it humbly asked to be allowed to make single copies of old sound and film recordings, since the then proposed extension of the 50-year music copyright to 95 years meant the certain destruction of most of the British Library Sound Archive.[17] Moreover, what it allows the British public to access for free, it sometimes sells to commercial interests abroad.

Only those scholarly fields which few professors, let alone the public, understand, are public domain. High-energy physics and molecular biology are open to all. But 20th century scholarship in the humanities and social sciences remains locked away by "The Sonny Bono Copyright Term Extension Act of 1998" (also known as the

---

[16]   A 2006 European Union directive stipulates copyright protection for life plus 70 years for authors of literary, artistic, cinematographic, and audiovisual works. EUR-Lex, "Directive 2006/116/EC of the European Parliament and of the Council of 12 December 2006 on the term of protection of copyright and certain related rights (codified version)": http://eur-lex.europa.eu/LexUriServ. do?uri=CELEX:32006L0116:EN:NOT. Literary works mean more than just fiction. The EU directive refers to "the rights of an author of a literary or artistic work within the meaning of Article 2 of the Berne Convention". Article 2 of the Berne Convention states, "The expression 'literary and artistic works' shall include every production in the literary, scientific and artistic domain, whatever may be the mode of form of its expression, such as books, pamphlets and other writings; lectures, addresses, sermons and other works of the same nature; dramatic or dramatico-musical works; choreographic works and entertainments in dumb show; musical compositions with or without words; cinematographic works to which are assimilated works expressed by a process analogous to cinematography; works of drawing, painting, architecture, sculpture, engraving and lithography; photographic works to which are assimilated works expressed by a process analogous to photography; works of applied art; illustrations, maps, plans, sketches and three-dimensional works relative to geography, topography, architecture or science." World Intellectual Property Organisation." Berne Convention for the Protection of Literary and Artistic Works: http://www.wip. int/treaties/en/ip/berne/trtdocs_wo001.html#P85_10661. EU copyright protection is automatic and does not need to be formally registered. BUYUSA.GOV, U.S. Commercial Service, "Copyright Protection in the European Union:" http:// www.buyusa.gov/europeanunion/ipr_copyright.html.
[17]   Undated pamphlet: picked up at the British Library, "Intellectual Property: A Balance: The British Library Manifesto".

"Micky Mouse Protection Act").[18] Look at the academic journal collection, JSTOR (if you can). Here you find the foundational work of the social sciences and the humanities – all closed to the public. The opportunity costs for society are self-evident. The public is rewriting knowledge through Wikipedia and the like. Should these sites not be hyperlinked with JSTOR?[19] By excluding the public from scholarly literature, copyright laws prevent amateurs from using sound research methodologies.

But what about the opportunity cost for scholars and the reputational risk for universities? The web tech community is working on how to verify information on the web, to "engineer layers of trust and provenance." The question is not whether the web will become scholarly in some meaningful sense. It is whether twentieth-century scholarship will be integrated into the scholarly world of the web.[20] Will universities become bystanders in the world of open access knowledge?[21]

If scholars hide away and lock up their knowledge, do they not risk their own irrelevance? Today's academics fail to engage with their immediate constituency (and former students): journalists, business leaders, professionals, politicians and civil servants. Yet these people house and feed professors. Is it not in universities' interests to let the educated bourgeoisie, and indeed the public at large, even look at, say, the Index of Christian Art?

---

[18]   To be compared to the first British copyright statue, the Statue of Anne in 1710, which set copyright at fourteen years, renewable only once. The need to renew copyright was removed in the US in 1992, and additionally copyright has become an assumed (rather than to be asserted) right.

[19]   Look up, for example, the eminent historian Natalie Zemon Davies in Wikipedia. The bibliography is good. But few of the entries are blue (linkable). Then look up, say, typhus, or any other major illness. You can hyperlink to recent medical research—but only rarely to the history of medicine references.

[20]   The Research Blogging website, started by Seed Media Group, aggregates and indexes posts on peer-reviewed data, and allows them to be tagged with metadata enabling priority of publication (*The Economist*, 20 September 2008, p. 96). The Transparent Accountable Datamining Initiative is at MIT and has a wide remit. The DBpedia project was started at the Free University (Berlin) and Leipzig University. It semantically queries the infobox templates embedded in Wikipedia's (English) articles (2.3 million of them, as of late 2008). Nigel Shadbolt and Tim Berners-Lee, "Web Science Emerges," *Scientific American*, October 2008, p. 65 and passim.

[21]   I borrow the concept of cultural agoraphobia from James Boyle at Duke University, and from a lecture he gave at Cambridge University Library on 12 March 2009, entitled "Cultural Agoraphobia and the Future of the Library".

¤ ¤ ¤ ¤

Half a millennium ago, German town folk were dazzled by the thought that, thanks to their new-fangled printing presses, God's word would now be put in the hands of the laity. There would be no need for intermediaries. God's word would speak, not through the clergy, but to each humble soul.

Of course the intermediaries struck back – the Counter-Reformation was arguably just that, a rebellion of intermediaries. But the technological rupture of the printing press was such that disintermediation was inevitable over the *longue durée*. We became – and look closely at the word – Protestants.

Today, at the dawn of the age of electronic reproduction, the intermediaries are again striking back. The publishers are the most blatant and crude. But academics are also intermediaries, and they too are striking back: university libraries are closed shops, JSTOR remains blocked, theses are inaccessible, and academic monographs are available only on paper and at prohibitive prices.

The obstacles to a true and electronic Reformation are real, but to be found also in "business as usual," a reluctance to imaginatively re-draw practices, and tear down organisational and legal "silos". Remember Henry Ford's comment: "If I had asked my customers what they wanted, they would have asked for a better horse carriage."

Obstacles can delay, but not stop, a technological rupture of this magnitude. Our children – always on, multi-tasking, mobile – will not engage with a body of scholarship their elders have incomprehensibly surrounded by barbed wire. But they will remain engaged in learning. The question is not whether there will be future scholars. It is how these future scholars will remember and integrate previous scholarship. And in pondering that, which means pondering the scholarly legacy of our age, it is worth remembering that "the generational war is the one war whose outcome is certain."

Why Copyright remains Important:
A Perspective from a Data Publisher

TREVOR FENWICK

CHAIRMAN, DATA PUBLISHERS ASSOCIATION, MANAGING
DIRECTOR, EUROMONITOR

Trevor Fenwick has over 30 years experience of the global business infor-
mation market as Managing Director of Euromonitor International, the
leading data publisher of market research analysis and reference data-
bases.. Based in the UK, has offices in Chicago, Singapore, Shanghai,
Vilnius, Dubai, Cape Town, Santiago, Sydney, and Tokyo.

Chairman of the Data Publishers Association, an ex-President of the Euro-
pean Association of Directory and Database Publishers he has been
directly involved with representing the business information sector's views
on intellectual property and data protection to UK government and the
European Commission since 1990. Trevor is a member of the Publishers
Content Forum, and a past member of the Legal Deposit Advisory Panel
and the Advisory Panel on Public Sector Information. He represents the
DPA onof the Advertising Association's Council.

He holds a degree in Economics and Government, postgraduate qualifica-
tions in marketing and is a Fellow of the Chartered Institute of Marketing.
He is a Liveryman of The Worshipful Company of Stationers and Newspa-
per Makers.

Abstract: Data publishing, where professional content is created, selected, collated and delivered as databases to professional and academic users has been a major adopter of
digital technology.

Data publishers are now also business service providers and
software applications designers. User agreements typically
rely in the first instance on Copyright law to protect that
investment but increasingly contracts include user specific
terms and conditions and licences reflecting the bespoke
nature of the relationship.

At the same time digitally enabled copying of music and
audiovisual has led to pressure to recognise this through
modifying existing copyright legislation.

Data publishers find themselves in a dilemma, on the one hand seeking additional protection for investment in database structures, content and delivery platforms yet on the other seeking to allow legitimate users access to and use of technical and professional information.

New business models are emerging which reflect the disintermediating impact of digital technology on traditional intermediaries including publishers, bookseller and libraries.

Why copyright remains important
A perspective from a data publisher

The debate on copyright has been brought about and dominated by a discussion of the issues surrounding consumer use and re-use of content, usually music, film or video, more often than not obtained digitally.

There is, however, a significant and no less important sector of the UK creative economy where copyright is as relevant but one which has had little recognition or consideration in the discussion on the importance of copyright in the digital economy.

This sector is part of the publishing universe occupied by data publishing, specifically professional, academic and business information publishing, the world of "need to know" rather than" nice to know".

In this part of the publishing world content is created and published to inform rather than entertain the user. This is a changing market; publishers now create and own the content and are increasingly software developers, service providers and systems integrators and the role of librarians, as the purchasers and gatekeepers but rarely the final user of the content, is threatened by the growth of near universal internet access and the impact of search engines.

Data publishers have invested heavily in the transition to digital publishing and distribution of content but are caught in the crossfire of a debate which takes little account of the complexities, legal and technical, of a market where content is delivered to be used and copied.

However the debate remains largely focused on issues of whether copying by consumers is "criminalising" the millions of downloaders and file sharers. These activities are only "illegal" if they lead to commercial piracy. The emotion, deliberately, generated by the "copy-left" protagonists ignores the damage which any general relaxation of copyright would do to most of the creative industries. In focussing on these populist aspects of the debate many important issues do not get the serious discussion they deserve.

Those promoting this debate are not without their own economic self-interest. The advent of the digital economy has created more opportunities than threats. Internet service providers (ISP's) and search engines are dependent on access to or the distribution of free-flowing content for the success of their businesses. The, often, unauthorised diversion of remuneration, as a result of reduced content sales or advertising revenues, from the rights-holder to the service provider or ISP is not sustainable if new, quality content is to continue to be produced and made available. Libraries are also increasingly active in this debate as they seek to protect their role of information disseminators as users stay away from physical establishments. The actions of libraries, in seeking further IP exceptions, should be seen in this context as part of a self-preservation policy to compete with the increased use of search engines, who have not respected IP rights to the same extent as libraries, as a means of finding and accessing information.

What is being protected? Creativity, expressions of ideas, yes; but the investment in the creation of factual data and the indexes, schemas and metadata structures are no less creative and involve no less an investment than that necessary to create a piece of literature or music. Are the investments in these essential parts of the creative process of data publishing properly protected?

Data Publishing ... Copyright, creativity and investment in factual content

It is important not to confuse the business challenges facing "info-mediaries" (publishers, printers, libraries and search engines) with a failure of copyright.

Data publishers are at the leading edge of a shift in the value chain. Whilst content creators are and continue to be preeminent it is now publishers and other elements in the distribution chain who are challenged. The history of publishing can be viewed as the story of the impact of changing technologies on how the written word is communicated. The Statute of Anne in 1710 recognised the rights and claims of content creators as opposed to the owners of the then dominant technology, printing, and in doing so enabled publishing to prosper. As new technologies evolve they invariably cause stresses in existing business models. In the last twenty years technology has been in the ascendancy. There is now a growing realisation that technology without content or technology which destroys content creation is unsustainable .Technology companies recognise this and have started to acquire content, initially with disregard to the rights-holders' interests, by any means to satisfy the appetite of their applications for deep and rich content.

Business models are rapidly changing to reflect the impact of those technologies. In this digital world those involved in the "traditional" publishing value chain of content creation (authors), selection, the adding of value through the payment of advances and guarantees, application of financial and intellectual capital such as branding editorial interaction, design, printing and marketing (publishers) and distribution (retailers and librarians) have all been, to greater or lesser extent, affected by the impact of new technology. The current debate is part of the process of the rights-holders and users to establish those new business models and achieve a fair balance of rights to access and use which does not undermine the legitimate economic rights of the rights-holders.

Authors have been empowered by these changes. Self-publishing, digital marketing and promotion in the print and music sectors have enabled authors to build their own businesses and achieve advancement in their professions. Some of these content creators have taken a less rigid approach to copyright, taking the view that building a reputation by allowing copying will allow revenue streams to be developed in other areas. These dynamic new business models are challenging the traditional publishing models.

Traditional publishing has been severely challenged by digital technology. Lack of anticipation and lethargic reaction has meant that many consumer facing publishers (fiction, non-fiction, magazines and newspapers) are struggling to adapt to and rebuild revenue streams in a world where content is accessed online (legally and illegally), advertisers are paying search engines rather than content owners, traditional routes to market (high street booksellers) are challenged by supermarkets and online retailers and broadcasters, some using public funding, are offering comprehensive alternative free at point of access content offerings.

Publishers of business, technical and academic content, although subject to the same macro changes, have turned these changes to their advantage. The changes brought about by the development of digital technology to create, organise and deliver content direct to users are an early indicator of the benefits that can be derived in this exciting new world.

In this information sector content is still created, usually by authors but increasingly by selection and arrangement of empirical data systematically collected from external data sources, with other data and content, licensed or freely available from public sources, normalised, aggregated and delivered to users with software and access interfaces allowing users to select and arrange the content to met their specific needs.

Copyright protects the rights of the creator to enjoy an exclusive right on their creativity. Ideas are not copyright only the expression of the idea. Facts are held to be beyond copyright. Yet what is a fact? Some are obvious, names and addresses, others less so. Statistics and data, other than those established by empirical measurement, are often held to be facts. This is rarely the case; statistics are no less the result of a creative process than any other copyright work. In reality most facts are estimations based on samples adjusted and calibrated by an analyst. The production of statistics and data is no less a creative process than the production of any other form of copyright material. It is ironic that the most successful copyright defence tool data publishers have been able to deploy is that of implanting erroneous data, a false name or made up address, into a database.

In the data publishing world the investment costs of data collection, aggregation, normalisation and analysis are high. Specialist data sets are expensive to produce yet often are targeted at a small user community.

Databases are nowadays rarely simple collections of otherwise published materials bundled together, as in an anthology, to which the publisher adds some search and retrieval software. Increasingly databases are sophisticated amalgams of data (historic, compiled, newly created, licensed) from selected sources. The data is validated, normalised and aggregated. Active, dynamic links to external data sources (text, audio visual) are often included. Metadata is produced, allowing the information to be precisely selected, in order to meet the users' specific needs. Usage and access monitoring technologies are embedded to allow subscriber access depending on the business model (free access or subscription) and specific user requirements. The data is then compiled into a database which works with specific delivery platforms to enable access.

Data publishers are increasingly working directly with users to determine what features of the database and its functionality are required. The interfaces and access applications provided by the data publisher are growing in importance as being part of the reason that users select and pay for access and use of a publisher's content and service offering. Customer defined selections and applications allow additional user generated content and third party applications to be integrated into a common interface precisely tailored to each individual subscriber organisation's needs and requirements.

In these situations simple reliance on copyright by itself, is no longer realistic. Copyright, of course, remains the basis of the relationship between creator and user for the reason that it is the right to use that copyright which is being contracted and licensed. A rightsholder may take an action against a user for breach of contract or licence but this is only valid if there is an enforceable right in copyright. Users pay for access to a database because of the added value its use gives to their organisation. That relationship is normally contract based which typically reflects copyright but further recognises the specific uses the purchaser wants to apply that content to. Increasingly the delivery and maintenance of these services are ongoing business relationships. Unlike the sale of a book or a journal subscription where a simple invoice and reliance on the ongoing general provisions of copyright law would usually suffice, these new business relationships involve long term contracts, service level agreements, usage terms and conditions. Contract and licensing law is now as important in this as copyright law.

The growth in the use of research data by commercial enterprises was recognised in the 2003 Copyright Act. Copyright law had accrued a number of exceptions which allow copying to take place under certain limited and specified circumstances. For UK data publishers the most relevant is "fair dealing for research and private study" (not to be confused with its distant and rather different US cousin "fair use"). The 2003 Copyright Act, which implemented the EU Information Society Directive, recognised the abuse of this fair dealing provision and amended Section 29 of the 1998 Copyright Design and Patents Act to include the words "non-commercial":

> *"Fair dealing with a literary, dramatic, musical or artistic work for the purposes of research for a non-commercial purpose does not infringe any copyright in the work provided that it is accompanied by a sufficient acknowledgement."*

Added protection for Databases

Today's data products deliver considerable added value and user benefits over and above print products. Data services are accessed, read, used and reused. They are as much a part of commercial investment as the financial and human resources which are essential to modern investment decisions. Business, reference and academic information is by nature different in that it has the potential and intention to be used commercially. The more it is used the greater the value the user attaches to it and the greater the ability of the content provider to invest and develop further successful services.

The need to protect this investment, that is the investment over and above that of the creation of the underlying content, was recognised by the European Union with the publication of the Database Directive in 1996. The implementing legislation protects databases in two ways; firstly a database may qualify for protection as a copyright work; a second, Sui Generis, right recognises that some databases will be protected as the result of the substantial investment in the obtaining, verification or presentation even though they have no copyright. This value of this legislation in recognising the investment in the database as a whole, the Sui Generis right, has, as the result of complex and apparently conflicting judicial decisions, been questioned. This is unfortunate as this is an important legislative recognition of the need to protect investment in collecting and arranging content which may not of itself have the protection of copyright.

As "data publishers" become "information providers" they generate intellectual property beyond that of original content (factual or not). The database as a whole may enjoy either or both of the rights recognised by the Database Directive but the creation of schemas and metadata which describe and help to order data are in them creative acts resulting from significant investment and are in themselves worthy of protection from unauthorised copying and utilisation for commercial purposes.

Access to and reuse of information through libraries

The new order is challenging the traditional role of libraries. Just as publishers are having to adopt new business models so too are traditional libraries ; wider societal internet access keeps an ever increasing number of users away from libraries and as screen based communication erodes reading as a leisure activity and as a means of accessing factual and reference information.

The traditional role of the librarian as benevolent custodian of publisher materials is increasingly being questioned by publishers of high value products as libraries strive to maintain their role by giving access to digital content. This is particularly the case in libraries which serve the research and academic community. At a time when copyright is generally disregarded by users who have become accustomed to the ease of copying, albeit usually illegal, of digital consumer content, libraries are faced with the difficulty of policing access to high value content. The potential for conflict of interest is unavoidable and results in libraries now being both the source of much of the illegal copying of high value content and at the same time the source of the greatest pressure for the further relaxation of copyright by the increase in the scope of library exceptions and moves to prevent the use of licences to regulate user access.

This part of the debate is brought into sharp focus by the deployment by publishers of increasingly sophisticated processes, technological and contractual, to monitor and control access to their services to ensure use is compliant with the publishers' user agreements'.

The use of this technology is a bone of contention for librarians, yet it is libraries which are, for high value data publishers, the increasingly leaky bucket as the source of data being misappropriated for purposes which damage the economic rights of the publisher. For example:

A rival publisher accesses a competitor's content by registering as business user at a business school library. The publisher's researchers systematically download large sections of the database and republish it as their own. They are exposed when the original publisher's clients recognise content through seeded data, and deliberate misspellings which have been repeated.

A publisher's usage monitoring system identifies high volume usage by a European university student user ID at a European university from an internet cafe in India. The university library confirms that the user access account is registered to a foreign student whose home address is India. The student does not to respond e-mails and fails to return to the University to continue studies.

These cases highlight the difficulties faced by librarians and publishers alike in dealing with this problem. The reality is that, in a world where the disregard of copyright is now commonplace in all user communities, technological measures to control measure and regulate access are necessary.

In competing with the internet availability of content and the increasing functionality of search engines libraries are having to address own raison d'être and are developing new business models which risk a breakdown in the trust relationship long enjoyed with publishers. The concerns of the publishing community over access and use of digital publications through the extension of legal deposit reflects this concern.

Copyright (plus)?

At a Creative Economy Conference in London in 2006 the importance of copyright was recognised:

> *"Copyright is crucial. In this new era, everything becomes a subset of Intellectual Property. We believe that copyright has been a highly effective mechanism to generate creative wealth in the industrial mechanical age, and the concepts of copyright will continue to do so as they adapt to the online era."*

If Marshall McLuhan were writing today he may well have come to a different conclusion; not that it is the "Medium which is the Message "but rather it is the "Medium which needs the Message".

The continued growth in digital media is dependent on content. The higher the quality the better the chances of market success through user demand. New technologies come and are in turn replaced by newer technologies which will thrive until the next new technology arrives. These technologies only succeed because of the content they facilitate access to. The demand for high quality content has never been greater and the need for protection of the investment of the creative industries to enable that high quality content to continue to be produced is, equally, as necessary as it ever was.

Copyright remains fit for purpose in enabling that which Queen Anne intended: "the encouragement of learning" and "to enable learned men to compose and write useful books".

Data publishers surely "do" just that ... create "useful" content sets and facilitate access to data.

Copyright does not lock up content; it protects the right of the content creator to secure a return on the investment in creating that content. It is an economic right and the redress allowed under UK law is the loss of profit suffered as a result of the infringement. If the damage is not substantial the redress will not be substantial but the prevention of further, greater infringements may be prevented.

Content remains king but technology is, as it ever was, the king maker. Creators of content must have the right to protect their investment. Copyright ensures a universally applicable "ground zero", a safety net for all content creators whilst still protecting users' rights. Yet in a fragmented and increasingly technologically enabled media world, specialist applications and uses need further protection.

Data publishers combine high quality content, data structures, software and access systems creatively engineered to meet users' specific needs. If this activity is not protected by copyright the publishers and users must be free to negotiate licences, contracts and user agreements that meet the needs of all parties whilst recognising the fundamental and important protections of copyright.

Other Men's Flowers

DAVID R WORLOCK

David Worlock is a Cambridge History graduate who joined Thomson Reuters as a trainee in 1967, and subsequently worked in educational and academic publishing before managing Thomson's school-based publishing as Group Executive Publisher in the late 1970s. Between 1980-85 he was CEO of the pioneer development of EUROLEX, the UK's first online service for lawyers, subsequently acquired by Reed Elsevier in 1985. In that year he founded Electronic Publishing Services Ltd, a research and consultancy company based in London and New York which has worked alongside the digital content industry in developing strategies for products and markets in consumer and business sectors. Content environments have ranged from text to audio-visual, from online to wireless, from narrowband to broadband. Major projects included the development of Fish4 of which he was non-executive chairman for five years. Public consultancy work includes advisory services and projects for the European Commission, the Department of Trade and Industry, the British Library, QCA and the Soros Foundation.

Abstract: A sub-culture of illicit content re-use has always undermined legal protection of copyright. In the digital network that sub-culture becomes the dominant style of usage. Publishers need a new business model based on value added to content , and the network needs a framework of implied and actual licensing to allow users to behave as they are now empowered to behave. Ownership and the right to be named as the original source of content must be clear but attempts to control re-use once content is introduced into the Open Web will simply bring the law further into disrepute

Other Men's Flowers

Of the making of anthologies there is no end. While few have the eminence of General Lord Wavell's effort, whose title stands at the head of this page, the seven that I saw through the press for their schoolmaster compilers as a junior editor in an educational publishing house between 1967 and 1970 no doubt fulfilled their historic role of filling lesson space, providing homework learning-by-heart, boring the already terminally bored, and, once or twice, striking a note of intellectual excitement or amusement that turned a young mind on to something different. My editorial mentors were skilled at the copyright clearance game. " No George Orwell, mind, that Sonia Brownell won't allow discounts for school books", " Plenty of Out of Copyright " (when did George Gissing die?), and " try to quote where you can within the meaning of the Act" (how much of a poem makes a breach ?).

My most successful effort, in 1969, was a low budget production called Conflict 1, selling for £1.25, with a budget for copyright fees of £95.00. I got inside the budget (there is a great deal of children's own verse in it), the brilliant compilers at Eltham Green School hit paydirt (or as much as you can on 2.5% of net sales after discounts!) as an examination set book, and the fees charged by agents for Conflict 2 and 3 when they appeared skyrocketed.

However, the samizdat manuscripts of pirated content that the compilers had been copying for use in class or circulation via advisors to other schools went legitimate for the first time. We did not have the internet but we did have community and, with it, the sharing of content within communities in defiance of legal restraint.

In fact, our great complaint then was that we publishers were using the law as the law was intended to be used but no one else was. We produced posters to put on the wall alongside school photocopiers drawing the attention of teachers to the fair use provisions of the Act, but whenever I spoke to teachers they were unrepentant about copying what they needed " in the interests of education".

And so, in a sense, was I, who had also entered educational publishing to help to make a difference, whether that was in SE London, or Lagos or Nairobi. In the two latter places they did not then have photocopiers so they were within the law, but suffered from a grave lack of books. In London they also needed more books, but they could take action and defy the law to meet their needs and get within their budgets. We all knew that we were on a slippery anarchistic slope, and some of us presumed, sometimes with a frisson of excitement, that the slope would end up at a cliff edge, and we would go right over. Others simply assumed that law would be self-reforming: no society can live permanently with laws that much or even most of society disregard in ordinary life, and that inevitably, but after the fact, legal provision would re-align with the way in which citizens want to live.

Between 1970 and the mid-nineties yawns a gulf of enforcement inactivity and publisher complaints about the erosion of their control/margins. By 1979 I was a digital publisher, licensing legal information into searchable databases (and learning that much of the law is outdated and unenforceable), and by the mid-nineties I was running a consultancy business to advise publishers on going to the network. As with CD-ROM, we rushed at the technology and promptly reproduced within it all of the material which we had harboured in print, then sold it more cheaply and in a more easily reproducible form. And we as publishers stuck rigidly to our formats, product definitions and product pricing.

Some cheered when DotCom boom turned to Bust

Some of my clients secretly cheered when the DotCom boom turned to Bust, and anticipated a return to the apparent security and pretence of control offered by print, conveniently forgetting their earlier complaints that they were losing control of that. They were particularly dismayed when Bust turned to Boom again, but this time with a real twist. This time the patients had taken over the asylum. This time the network began to mean co-operation and collaboration.

Despite the silly name, Web 2.0 really is a turning point. My schoolteacher friends, were they still at Eltham Green, would be anthologizing on the Web, sending and discussing the results with pupils, adding and editing all the while, and not addressing the legitimate concerns of Miss Sonia Brownell and A M Heath at any point. They would not even know, or perhaps care, that the law has changed many times in the meanwhile, that educational fair use is far better defined, or that the library lobby has won ground against the publishers. The only salient fact is this : they can do it, so they will do it.

It is conventional to talk about print copyright by using as examples the music and video industries, and point to the disasters and recoveries attendant upon their encounters with the digital world. I would contend that the progression outlined here indicates that we only need to look within the print world to see where we are going, and that the future landscape for copyright now appears before us with awful clarity. The publisher in the network has been sidelined as the controller of content formatting. He will continue to exist in the developing role of ringmaster, but in a context where the active element of web presence – working in a business process, participating as a learner in a virtual classroom, booking a holiday – require content support to complete their functionality.

And so the traditional publisher morphs into an entrepreneurial repackager of content needed for work, or study or entertainment in situations where, using software or the anthologer's science of selection and licensing, he is able to bring additional value into the game which people will pay for and which will create a margin. But you do not have to be a former print publisher to fulfil these roles : internet service companies, enterprise software companies, schools and teachers, private individuals et al can fulfil them. And we cannot even look to the ancilliary revenue streams created by advertising as a way of retaining a publishing position in a traditional sense, since it is now becoming clear that advertising too is changing its nature and its dominance in the collaborative network where community endorsement may be more valuable to the advertiser than the ability to shower us all in unwanted and intrusive messaging.

Rights attached to content ownership get bent and buckled

In this networked world the nature and rights attached to content ownership get bent and buckled too. To the secret joy of competition lawyers, who have always hated monopoly rights, copyright will be denuded into simple statements of origination, the right to be named as the originator, and the right not to release content into network use.Recognition and ownership are unlikely to outlive authors.But there is certainly a place for Creative Commons style provisions here. Once content is released to the Open Web it will be difficult to claim re-use fees of any type. Some content will always be Dark Web (indeed there are currently signs that this is growing) but Open Web content will increasingly be held in common without effective barriers to re-use. This will take a long time in some instances (in science publishing, for example, it is likely that the nature of scholarly communication itself and within it a change in the place of the research article, will be more important than the current advocacy for Open Access and the removal of ownership controls on journal content). And the Web will become a place of real or implied licences, with standardized payments via collection agency toll-based systems becoming the normal – or only – way of securing any form of second use recompense.

Society and the Web mirror each other exactly. There is no accident in the rise of global and local digitally-networked community access. Our former magazine and book publishing customers seek the like–minded on the Web and express the need to communicate with them in the network. In order to do that they need content, but the content harboured by real world publishers and sold at a price will become commoditized, or be "emulated", if we insist on using legal provisions derived from a pre-networked world to protect it. The problem of the network and its communities will not be too little content, with publishers refusing to allow it outside of the Dark Web : it will be too much content, with users making their own, emulating protected material, or "outing" copyright material so widely that it becomes as commonplace as a Pamela Anderson movie on the Web in the late 1990s. And those who "re-use" without permission will claim the justification of Art : historically copyright content will become a part of someone's collage, integrated into web anthologies which are themselves creative works, re-used so widely that no one any longer can guess the source. One of the greatest problems of the world, where each and every one of us is a publisher, may be in providing authenticity and giving authentication. This may be a major part of the future history of libraries in the network.

Meanwhile, the true concentration of erstwhile publishers should not be ownership or protection of content, but added value and service provision. As content becomes more and more commoditised (Google is now a major publisher of primary legal information) so we move up the value chain. There will be problems about protecting ownership in that field as well. Better we concentrate on those, and on effective licensing schemas, than waste more time on law reform in the copyright area. That horse has bolted, and even the stable door has begun to rust away from long disuse.

An Act for the Encouragement of ... Enforcement

RODERICK KIRWAN

PARTNER DENTON WILDE SAPTE

Roderick leads the Communications group in the Technology, Media and Telecoms department of Denton Wilde Sapte. He provides commercial and regulatory advice to suppliers, operators, online service providers and users of fixed and mobile communication networks. He has particular experience of internet and on-line services, mobile networks, telecommunications and online regulatory law and electronic cash payment systems. He has considerable experience in large international internet and communication projects and regularly works for clients in Europe, Africa and the Middle East.

Abstract: The world's first copyright law was passed in 1710 as "an act for the Encouragement of Learning". The Digital Economy Act 2010[1] (DEA) became law on the final day of the 2009-10 parliamentary session, and is intended to update enforcement of copyright in an online world.

The DEA was steered through the Houses of Commons and Lords by Ben Bradshaw (Secretary of State for Culture, Media and Sport) and Lord Mandelson (Secretary of State for Business, Innovation & Skills) respectively. The DEA implements some of the policy aims set out in Lord Carters' Digital Britain Report,[2] including in new provisions designed to enhance copyright protection against illegal file-sharing and on-line piracy. This article explains the key anti-piracy provisions of the DEA and considers its impact for content owners, internet service providers and individual internet users.

---

[1] http://www.opsi.gov.uk/acts/acts2010/ukpga_20100024_en_1
[2] http://www.culture.gov.uk/images/publications/digitalbritain-finalreport-jun09.pdf

An Act for the encouragement of ... enforcement

A controversial Act

The road to royal assent for the Digital Economy Act (DEA) of 2010 was controversial. Only a series of trades on contentious issues allowed the Labour government to secure passage of the DEA at all. Bradshaw and Lord Mandelson had to give up provisions dealing with the funding of Channel 4, local news provision and super-fast broadband networks to achieve the intended copyright reforms. And critics voiced procedural concerns over the lack of detailed scrutiny of the legislation resulting from the use of parliament's pre-election 'wash-up' procedure, and practical concerns over the influence of lobbying from the music industry in the forming of policy and the drafting of the DEA.

Although the DEA deals with a range of digital economy issues (including Ofcom's role, internet domain registries, Channel Four's future, regulation of TV and radio, spectrum use, and public lending) most attention has focused on provisions dealing with online copyright infringement. Media interest was spiked by a war of words between representatives of rights-holders (supportive of the DEA) and ISPs and internet freedom pressure groups (who oppose its provisions).

Cutting off broadband for persistent copyright pirates

Although opponents secured limited concessions as the DEA ping-ponged between Lords and Commons, rights-holders scored a key victory with the introduction of a new framework to establish anti-piracy measures. Depending on the extent of online copyright infringement in the next 12-18 months, further legislative action under that framework could ultimately lead to ISPs having to take technical steps (including bandwidth throttling and account suspension) against subscribers whose internet connections are persistently used for copyright infringement.

This framework is established through a series of amendments to section 124 of the Communications Act 2003.[3] The amendments allow rights-holders to make reports to ISPs detailing suspected copyright infringement by ISPs' subscribers. On receiving a report an ISP must notify the affected subscribers. Rights-holders can require ISPs to provide them with anonymised lists showing which

---

[3]   http://www.opsi.gov.uk/ACTS/acts2003/ukpga_20030021_en_1

of their infringement reports relate to which subscribers (thus high-lighting persistent infringement).

These actions will have to be in accordance with an 'initial obligations code', agreed by the industry or, in default of industry agreement, created by Ofcom and approved by the Secretary of State. Some of the content of this code of practice is specified, at a high level, in the DEA. For instance, the code must include details of robust appeal mechanisms, costs allocation between rights-holders and ISPs and a requirement for a court order before infringing subscriber details are passed to an ISP. Once the code is in force, Ofcom will have to prepare quarterly and full annual reports detailing the extent of online copyright infringement. If the first annual report shows online copyright infringement is not reducing as a result of the 'infringement notification' mechanism set out in the code the Secretary of State will be able to direct Ofcom to assess whether "technical obligations" should be imposed on ISPs to take "technical measures" (such as bandwidth throttling or service suspension) against subscribers who persistently infringe copyright. Following that assessment the Secretary of State will be able, by order, to impose such "technical obligations" on ISPs. That order will have to be approved by both Houses of Parliament after at least 60 days for review. If such obligations are put in place Ofcom will have to put in place a code to regulate their exercise.

Although Ofcom could wait to see if industry puts in place an "initial obligations code" it appears to consider this unlikely with good reason, given past experience. It has already indicated that it will draft parts of the code and consult on the draft. Ofcom also plans to establish the methodology it will use to estimate levels of online copyright infringement and so set the benchmark against which to assess whether infringement notifications are successful.

Preventing access to locations on the internet

As well as for measures to cut off broadband access, vociferous criticism was levelled at sections 17 and 18 of the DEA. Those sections create the possibility of courts ordering the take-down of websites that might be used for copyright infringement.

The provisions allow the Secretary of State, by regulation, to put in place measures under which a copyright holder will be able to obtain a court injunction requiring ISPs to block access to a *"location on the internet which the court is satisfied has been, is being or is likely to be used for or in connection with an activity that infringes copyright"*.

The Secretary of State will only be able to put in place such measures if satisfied that they are a proportionate way to deal with the problem of online copyright infringement, and the regulations will have to contain detailed tests for the courts to apply before granting an injunction. Further, the Secretary of State will have to consult widely before presenting its reasons for thinking regulations are necessary, and there will have to be a 60-day period for parliamentary review before the Secretary of State can issue the regulations.

These provisions have raised fears that rights-holders might seek injunctions to close popular websites such as Google and Wikileaks. Both of those websites, on a broad interpretation, are locations on the internet which might be used in connection with an activity that infringes copyright, and therefore could be within the scope of regulations. While legislators have said the intent is not for those sorts of websites to be shut down, and any regulations put before Parliament will include protections, critics have suggested the better way to avoid secondary legislation that risks such intrusive results is not to create broad enabling primary legislation in the first place. Perhaps the most significant voice in the debate is that of Google itself. The search giant reacted to the DEA by saying: "we absolutely believe in the importance of copyright, but blocking through injunction creates a high risk that legal content gets mistakenly blocked, or that people abuse the system."

The copyright holder's view

Unsurprisingly, representatives of rights-holders have expressed strong support for the copyright infringement measures contained in the DEA. The BPI commented that *"the measures to reduce illegal downloading will spur on investment in new music and innovation in legal business models"*, while the Publishers Association said *"as publishers are increasingly investing in the creation and delivery of digital content, so the measures passed will help to secure that investment"*.

Giving effect to the DEA has practical difficulties acknowledged by rights-holders. In particular, methods for measuring the extent of illegal filesharing will prove difficult. Technology recently implemented by Virgin Media to track illegal filesharing is the subject of an EU investigation into claims that it breaches privacy law, following a complaint from Privacy International. That suggests finding a legitimate way to obtain the data necessary to determine whether illegal filesharing reduces is not an easy technical question. If Ofcom is not able to obtain the data then the Secretary of State will presumably struggle to justify exercising the power to make an order requiring ISPs to implement technical measures against persistent illegal file-sharers.

Other views

Criticism of the DEA has come from privacy and internet freedom pressure groups, and some ISPs and major websites. The Open Rights Group called the DEA an *"utter disgrace"*, arguing that it constitutes *"an attack on everyone's right to communicate, work and gain an education"*. Talk Talk said the DEA contained *"many draconian proposals"* and criticised the lobbying effort and the parliamentary procedure: *"this is made all the more appalling by the ability of big music and film companies to influence government and the absence of any proper debate or scrutiny by MPs"*. And O2 has suggested the DEA does not address the problem of the lack of innovative business models to tempt users away from illegal file-sharing, saying: *"new products and services should be developed to give consumers the content they want, how they want it, and for a fair price"*.

A different angle of attack has focused on possible unintended consequences of broadband account suspension. Critics of the DEA have argued that it risks punishing libraries, schools, and other institutions that make wi-fi available publicly, and that those bodies should not be expected to track and manage the activities of all possible users of their connections.

Critics have also made pragmatic objections. They point to a study by the BI Norwegian School of Management which suggests those who download music illegally are ten times more likely to be legal purchasers of music than those who don't. Journalists have questioned the accuracy of some of the statistics used by the music industry in calling for the implementation of the anti-piracy measures of the DEA:[4] one set of figures effectively ascribes a value of £25 to each individual illegal download in assessing the cost to the industry. The point they make is that illegal downloaders are among the best customers for music and their download activity does not displace sales to the extent claimed.

Conclusion

Any assessment of the DEA is academic at this stage. The DEA puts in place a framework for future action, rather than bringing immediate change. The anti-piracy provisions of the DEA are unlikely

---

[4] http://www.guardian.co.uk/commentisfree/2009/jun/05/ben-goldacre-bad-science-music-downloads

to have direct impact on individuals until 2012 at the earliest, and might not come into force if illegal file-sharing falls (or cannot be measured accurately). And it is unlikely that doomsday predictions of Google being blocked and businesses ending public wi-fi provision will come to pass any time soon, if at all.

The political dimension is also significant. During the election, the Conservatives made it clear that any legislation agreed in the wash-up (as the DEA was) will be subject to review if they win power, and may be repealed. The Liberal Democrats called for the DEA during the election campaign, saying: "it was far too heavily weighted in favour of the big corporations and those who are worried about too much information becoming available. It badly needs to be repealed, and the issues revisited".

Significantly, many of the most controversial aspects of the DEA require secondary legislation to become effective. Whether the Conservative-Liberal Democrat coalition has the inclination or appetite to bring in these secondary measures remains an open question.

Even if the measures become effective, the impact on file-sharing is uncertain. Sweden recently enacted similar legislation to cut-off broadband access for illegal file-sharers. Internet traffic fell by more than 30% after enactment of a anti-piracy law, reflecting a drop off in illegal file-sharing. However, subscribers quickly learnt to bypass detection of illegal file-sharing. Internet traffic exceeded the pre-legislation levels within 3 months of the anti-piracy law, only with subscribers encrypting their traffic to avoid prosecution.

The Role of the Creative Industries in Rebuilding the UK Economy

BY HELEN ALEXANDER

PRESIDENT OF THE CBI

Helen Anne Alexander CBE, was born on 10 February 1957. She was educated at St Paul's Girls' School, where she is now deputy chair of the Governors and chair of the Education Committee.

She obtained an MA from Hertford College, Oxford and became an Honorary Fellow in 2002. She obtained an MBA from INSEAD in 1984 and is currently chair of the Business Advisory Council of the Said Business School, Oxford University.

Helen began her publishing career at Gerald Duckworth and Faber & Faber. She moved to The Economist in 1985 as marketing manager. She became managing director of The Economist Intelligence Unit in 1993 and in 1997 became chief executive of The Economist Group. Helen was chief executive for 11 years until she stepped down in June 2008. She was awarded a CBE for services to publishing in 2004.

In addition to her experience at the helm of an international business, Helen also has extensive board experience across a range of sectors. She was a non-executive director at Northern Foods plc (1994-2002) and at BT plc (1998-2002). She is currently non-executive director and chair of the remuneration committee at Centrica plc (2003) and Rolls-Royce Group plc (2007).

In 2008, Helen became vice-president of the CBI and senior adviser to Bain Capital. Helen is also senior Trustee of the Tate Gallery and is married with three children.

This address was delivered as the Livery Lecture to the Stationers' Company, 8 March 2010

Abstract: As someone who has spent much of her career involved in publishing media, I believe strongly that publishing has a great future ahead of it, even if its appearance may be radically different as we adjust to the digital age.

I joined The Economist in 1985 as marketing manager, and spent a lot of time with the brand.

The Economist, internationally, in its consumer form, and with the Economist Intelligence Unit, the B2B arm, so I've been around since the emergence of digital delivery in our industry in the early 90s!

Publishing of all types constitute the largest of the creative industries[1] all of which have, I think, a considerable role to play in the rebuilding of our economy after the downturn. In this address I paint a picture of the shape different parts of the creative industries are in, and then ask what particular support or encouragement they might need to build on their position as one of the UK's great internationally competitive success stories.

The role of the creative industries in rebuilding the UK economy

What are 'the creative industries'?

As the name suggests, the creative industries create! I don't just mean that they create books, newspapers, magazines, films and all the rest of it. I mean too that they create jobs and careers. They help create our cultural identity and the social environment we live in. And they help create the wealth that our economy and society needs.

What do I mean by the creative industries? The Department for Culture, Media and Sport, which has responsibility here, has defined them as including: advertising; architecture; art and antiques; computer games; crafts; design; fashion; film and video; music; the performing arts; television and radio; and of course publishing.[2]

You may have your own views as to what should and shouldn't feature on this list, but let's stick to official lines for the time being. These creative industries grew at twice the rate of the economy as a whole between 1997[3] and 2004, averaging five per cent a year.

Even in the eye of the destructive economic storm we've just limped out of, the creative industries performed well. Analysis from NESTA suggests that they will have grown at around four per cent this year and last year, and will continue to grow at the same rate

---

[1]   http://www.culture.gov.uk/what_we_do/creative_industries/default.aspx
[2]   http://www.culture.gov.uk/what_we_do/creative_industries/default.aspx
[3]   and IPO (2009) The future: developing a copyright agenda for the 21 Century,) http://www.ipo.gov.uk/c-policy-consultation.pdf

until 2013 – that is more than double[4] the rate for the rest of the economy. By 2013, NESTA expects there to be around 180,000 creative businesses in the UK,[5] contributing as much as £85bn of added value to the economy – and 150,000 new jobs.

Already, there are almost two million people employed in the creative industries, both directly and in related businesses. They contribute more than eight per cent of GDP, whilst[6] the financial services sector represents about the same proportion.

This is a hugely important fact, and one that bears repetition and recognition! And raw figures aside, these industries define an image of Britain abroad and help shape a brand defined by imagination, excellence, inventiveness and style. Think Working Title, the Financial Times, Framestore and Burberry.

A day in the life of the creative industries

Let me add some more colour and give you some examples of how the UK creative industries are all around you. You wake up to the sound of the BBC Radio 4 Today programme, one of the best current affairs broadcast in the world. Or you might prefer Chris Evans on Radio 2, or any one of our commercial radio stations.

On your train journey to work, you listen to British bands like Coldplay or the Arctic Monkeys on your iPod, as designed by Londoner Jonathan Ive. And you read one of our national or regional newspapers, or one of the magazines British publishing is justly famed for.

You might work in a state-of-the-art building designed by those twin pillars of British architectural excellence, Norman Foster or Richard Rogers. Your taste in clothes might include home-grown designers like Paul Smith, Vivienne Westwood or Ozwald Boateng, even if your pocket can't always stretch to them.

You may well spend your free time enjoying the performing arts in London or Edinburgh, or visiting one of Britain's many antiques

---

[4]   NESTA (March 2009), Demanding Growth: why the UK needs a recovery plan based on growth and innovation,p.9, http://www.nesta.org.uk/library/documents/PP%2001%20020Demanding%20Growth%20print

[5]   Ibid p.13

[6]   IPO (2009) The future: developing a copyright agenda for the 21 Century, http://www.ipo.gov.uk/c-policy-consultation.pdf; http://www.statistics.gov.uk/downloads/theme_economy/BB09.pdf

markets and dreaming of the day when you get to make that successful bid at Sotheby's or Christie's.

Most of us here tonight might not be active computer gamers, but I bet plenty of your children or grandchildren will be fans of British-designed games like Tomb Raider or Grand Theft Auto. You might share with those children a love of Harry Potter, even if you assure your friends that you stick to the works of Salman Rushdie, Martin Amis or Ian McEwan.

And your family viewing may be dominated by Wallace & Gromit, Doctor Who and The Office, or any other of the visual treats that the BBC, ITV, Sky and Virgin bring us. Film buffs might escape to the cinema to watch a host of British stars in films made at the famous studios at Elstree, Shepperton or Ealing.

Of course I could go on and on. But the point is that some of the biggest, brightest and most successful brands and talents in the creative world are British-based, British-born or British-bred. And as befits our open economy, you do not have to be British to enjoy them!

Celebrating the creative industries

So that is my small celebration of our creative industries.

What I want to explore is whether we're giving them enough support and encouragement.

What else might they need to flourish? Do we even recognise many creative businesses as being proper businesses at all? Or do we think there is somehow something different about selling music or designer handbags compared to selling washing machines or travel insurance?

At some levels, I'm quite sure that there isn't. This is also about jobs, tax receipts and profit and loss, just as with any other part of the commercial world.

As CEO of the Economist Group, my performance was measured on shareholder return and performance in a financial sense. But – and there is a but – it was always clear that the special way we would achieve that would be by producing truly excellent products and services – in that case focussed on truly excellent independent journalism, with integrity.

Some challenges facing the creative industries are unique. What links many of them is that growth of the digital environment I've already mentioned. The ways in which we consume and share the creative industries' products is changing.

A world shaped by innovative companies like Google and Amazon undoubtedly brings with it massive and exciting opportunities. But, as is often the way, there are threats, too.

These industries are facing the dual pressures of structural change and cyclical downturn. For them to thrive, and to play their part in rebalancing the economy, we need to make sure government develops a coherent strategy to minimise those threats, and to get the environment for them right.

The first area to concentrate on is – piracy and protecting intellectual property.

Music and film piracy, online publishing rights, counterfeited goods and stolen designs are all sources of concern. We need to act on copyright and protect ourselves. Why, for example, are we the only major country that continues to allow camcorders in cinemas?

Illegal downloads are perhaps the biggest problem of all. The government says some seven million people in the UK download illegally.[7] Industry sources suggest only one in twenty songs downloaded is actually paid for.[8] Six in ten music filesharers in the UK also illegally download films.[9]

High-speed broadband is great if people are downloading legally but bad news if they aren't. The new generation of broadband access at 50 mega bits per second could allow the download of 200 MP3 music files in five minutes, a film in three and the complete digitised works of Charles Dickens in less than ten.[10]

There's a disturbing acceptance of this, to the extent that for many people, it is simply the way they get hold of entertainment.

When Radiohead released its album In Rainbows, it decided to offer it for free, with contributions on a voluntary basis. Yet despite

---

[7]   http://news.bbc.co.uk/1/hi/technology/8073068.stm
[8]   http://www.bis.gov.uk/the-future-of-the-creative-industries
[9]   International Federation of the Phonographic Industry (2010), IFPI Digital Music Report 2010
[10]   SABIP (May 2009) Copycats? Digital consumers in the online age http://www.sabip.org.uk/home/press/press-release/press-release-20090529.htm

this, more people downloaded it illegally through file-sharing networks than did so from the band's website.[11]

This may just have been habit, a result of familiarity with those networks. But it is clear evidence of a culture that needs to be challenged in order to ensure future viability.

Creative products of any sort can be expensive to produce. There's a lot of misses for every hit. And if the hits produced are being stolen, then there's no money to invest in the next wave of talent. The next Radiohead, the next Nick Park, the next J.K. Rowling, the next Russell T. Davies.[12]

Beyond film and the printed, spoken or sung word there are problems too. Counterfeiting designer goods is big business. And this is not just clumsily-produced goods with designers' names misspelt and crooked logos. The mass sale of counterfeit goods online requires co-ordinated, international action. The taking down of 1200 websites selling counterfeit goods in the UK in the run up to the festive period last year was a good start[13] but the government needs to build on this if there is to be a bright future for our designers.

We need a credible threat

To deal with digital piracy, a credible threat is needed. It may come through the Digital Economy Bill. However, the issues are complex and finding a solution is not straightforward. We don not have the answers, but we do know that the solution is going to have to have three features.

It will have to be fair, enforceable, and future-proof.

That is, fair to content owners AND distributors. Enforceable, recognising that expectations in this area have changed and we can't clog up the courts with this, and future-proof in that it is certain that, for example, tomorrow's peer to peer will be very different from today's, and there must be a democratic way to accommodate change.

---

[11] http://www.independent.co.uk/arts-entertainment/music/news/radiohead-sales-show-fans-loyalty-to-illegal-sites-884239.html

[12] Writer behind Queer as Folk and revitalised Doctor Who – http://en.wikipedia.org/wiki/Russell_T_Davies

[13] http://www.guardian.co.uk/money/2009/dec/03/police-shut-scam-shopping-websites

Legislation is an important backstop, but ultimately what we need is innovation to deliver the services to customers that they want, to consume in an easy and accessible way. The second thing we have to get right is regulation. The regulatory environment the creative industries operate in needs to respond, then, to the new world. Traditional market definitions are changing.

For example, there is now more advertising in the UK[14] on the internet than on television, and this is something that will challenge the competition authorities.

We need to get a regulatory philosophy which will allow us to compete globally, and allows competition at the smallest entry level. Regulation is currently constrained by national definitions, rather than international ones which might be more appropriate.

The new digital environment likewise is reshaping boundaries and this new market needs to be recognised in competition policy.

The nature of many of the products created by people in this room means that they can be consumed across the world by anyone in any place simply by accessing the internet. In this environment not only do we now have access to international markets, so companies from other countries have access to UK consumers.

Overregulation of UK companies compared to foreign competitors will place British creative industries at a disadvantage. Archie Norman, the new boss of ITV, recently said how frustrated he is with what he called the "inherited archaeology of regulation" in television, with structures such as contracts rights renewal, the mechanism that controls ITV1's advertising rates, still in place.[15]

One good example is the debate about product placement. Here in the UK, it has been illegal to use product placement on television, even though much programming is bought from countries like the US where this is not the case. All this means is that the money from the product placement audiences see does not go to our programme makers, but to theirs.

I am glad to say that product placement should soon be allowed now that European rules have changed and we have opted in to the change.

---

[14] http://www.guardian.co.uk/media/2009/sep/30/internet-biggest-uk-advertising-sector

[15] http://www.guardian.co.uk/media/2010/mar/03/bbc-cuts-itv-archie-norman

We welcome the Ofcom statement that they are looking to see if there are justifiable reasons to keep advertising restrictions. If there is not a public interest reason for keeping them, they'll get rid of them.[16] This overall presumption for deregulation unless there is a demonstrable issue that needs addressing is a very good one. I know you won't want to hear about regulation all night, so let us move on!

The third thing the government must get right for the creative industries is tax

The way the creative industries are taxed makes a difference. For the government the top priority is to reduce the national deficit, and there is a broad point about tax competitiveness. We do not want to see further evidence of talent and jobs and their tax-raising potential being lost overseas, as many fear will happen in the financial sector as the 50p income tax rate kicks in next month.

The creative industries, like others that have people at their heart, need to think about the cost of employing staff. So the increase in employer National Insurance contributions due in April 2011 is the exact opposite of what is needed if we are to create new jobs as well as protect and enhance existing ones.

We should also look carefully at the impact that other countries' policies are having on our creative industries. Canada has tax breaks for the computer games industry, recognising its potential for growth – and this is why it has overtaken the UK as the third-biggest games producer in the world.[17]

Here in the UK we do have film tax credits, and we are pleased that both main political parties have committed to their retention. France and Ireland have similar policies, and have enjoyed success as a result. The bigger point here is about recognising that tax matters for creative companies just as much as it does for the likes of pharmaceuticals and aerospace, not least in how they build intellectual property.

The CBI wants to see any future tax policy pass a test, which is: "Will it make the UK a more attractive place for businesses to invest in, develop and exploit IP?" We must have a stable and competitive tax framework if we are to incentivise IP development and exploitation. Change and uncertainty undermine the confidence of those making long- term investment decisions.

---

[16]   http://www.ft.com/cms/s/0/f1ea0d6e-2696-11df-bd0c-00144feabdc0.html
[17]   http://www.totalvideogames.com/TVG/news/PM-Praises-UK-Game-Industry-15010.html

We currently have a strong research and development tax credit scheme. But other countries are fast catching up, and are becoming more innovative in how they set tax structures to encourage IP development. We need to keep up the pace!

So that's piracy, regulation and tax.

Access to finance

For the creative industries to thrive they also need access to finance.

Keeping to the subject of money, access to finance is a particular issue for the creative industries, dominated as they are by SMEs. Medium-sized companies have found access to finance particularly hard to come by, and there is no indication this is easing greatly.

On top of this, there are risk factors involved that are peculiar to the creative industries. Music, films and books are not seen as safe bets – and so don not attract investment from banks keen to reduce their exposure to risk.

The government's Enterprise Finance Guarantee Scheme is meant to help alleviate this, but evidence on the ground from CBI members suggests this is not the case. To pick up on my earlier point, this is particularly damaging at a time when the traditional funding from within the industry is under threat as the music labels struggle under the onslaught of online piracy.

It is not all about money. Finance is not the only input the sector needs. Perhaps even more than any other, people are the creative industries' greatest asset. And for the future the creative industries need skills. Skills gaps are a particular focus of the CBI's work, and the biggest ones in recent times have been in science, technology, engineering and maths. We're understandably concerned that the proportion of young people studying these STEM subjects has fallen in the last decade, and by more than for most of our OECD competitors.[18]

And the point here is that STEM skills are not just needed to ensure we have enough engineers or lab technicians. The 'T' and the 'M' of technology and maths are important to the creative industries, too.

The computer games industry needs technology graduates and mathematicians. As I mentioned, the UK has the fourth-largest such

---

[18] http://www.totalvideogames.com/TVG/news/PM-Praises-UK-Game-Industry-15010.html

industry, and it needs good people to thrive and not slip further down the world rankings.[19] The same needs apply to many parts of the design and architecture worlds. Companies like Benoy, Zaha Hadid Architects and Arup need good people too. We need vocational skills as well, for example in fashion, crafts and film. The Pinewood Studios Group relies not only on a supply of top-notch film scripts, directors, actors and producers, but also on skilled trades people such as carpenters and drapers to bring the sets to life.

And as with other parts of the skills debate, there needs to be a relentless focus on employability. Ordinary things like turning up on time and other lessons need to be taught earlier, at college or university, not left to employers, who get frustrated with new employees' attitudes.

So it is a concern that the creative industries often lack adequate general business skills. I am loathe to mention creative accounting, especially with the play *Enron* enjoying a run in the West End, but a better understanding of even fairly basic financing methods, bookkeeping and office management is needed if more ideas are going to be translated into products.

Here intellectual property is again a consideration. IP is the basic currency of creative companies, and we must make sure people leaving education with first-class creative ideas and skills know how to protect or commercialise them. Members tell us that IP is not part of creative or even most business courses. The IP Institute is attempting to change this and is speaking to business schools to try to get this included in their programmes.

Conclusion

So these are some of the strands that need to be pulled together. Better IP protection. Helpful regulation. Improved access to finance. A competitive tax regime. The right skills.

The recalibration of the UK economy and the building of robust business growth in the years ahead need our creative industries to play an active and increasing role. We want to see far greater recognition of the creative industries and their significance. More coherent strategies are needed to realise the huge potential out there.

I believe the creative industries are a serious, grown-up, dynamic and innovative part of the British economy.

---

[19]   After the US, Japan and Canada – http://www.ukinvest.gov.uk/Feature/4032102/en-CA.html

I believe that they're a success story which all of us should be proud of, and the part they play in the economy is under-recognised. The CBI will call for recognition and will be doing all it can in the months and years ahead to tell this success story.

We will be a clear voice that can speak up for the whole sector whose diversity and breadth of activity is both a strength and sometimes a limitation. This is a critical part of UK plc that should and must be championed – must form part of the government's plans for a more balanced economy.

So thank you all for listening to me tonight, and thank you to the Stationers' Company for the opportunity to deliver your annual lecture. It's been a great honour.

The European Union: In 2010 is Copyright still able to Protect and Reward the Creative Heart of Europe?

ANGELA MILLS WADE

EXECUTIVE DIRECTOR, THE EUROPEAN PUBLISHERS COUNCIL

Since 1991 Angela Mills Wade has been the Executive Director of the European Publishers' Council (EPC), a high level group of Chairmen and CEOs of Europe's leading media groups representing companies with newspapers, magazines, online publishing, journals, databases, books and broadcasting. Since its formation the EPC has been communicating with Europe's legislatorson issues that affect freedom of expression, media diversity, democracy and the health and viability of media in the European Union.

Angela currently holds a number of industry and public appointments:

Chairman, UK Publishers Content Forum

Member of the UK Government's Legal Deposit Advisory Panel

Joint Chair (with the British Library) of the Joint Committee on Legal Deposit

Director and Member of the Project Board of ACAP (Automated Content Access Protocol)

Member of the External Advisory Board to Loughborough University's Department of Information Science

Vice-Chairman of the European Advertising Standards Alliance and Chairman of EASA's Media Committee

Member of the European Commission's Expert Group on Media Literacy

Chairman of Europe Analytica, an independent consultancy company based in Brussels

During her earlier career, Angela was the Head of European Affairs and Special Issues at the UK Advertising Association (1989 to 1991); European Executive for the ITV Companies' Association (1983 to 1987) and Assistant European Executive at the Retail Consortium (1980 to 1983). She represented these bodies on the Boards of their counter-part European level associations. Between 1977 and 1980 Angela worked for Davum Steel and Total Oil in London and for Forex Neptune in their Paris Office.

Angela is married with two children.

Abstract: Angela Mills Wade, Executive Director of the European Publishers Council explores the radically new views of Copyright in the internet world.

She examines how the European Union has dealt with copyright over recent years and is now approaching the conflict between some who assume almost everything on the web should be available for free and those who create content and publish it without whom that content would not exist.

In what form should content now be communicated, how labelled and how protected from inappropriate exploitation? What business models can publishers adopt and how can the future of professional journalism be secured? When competition for readers online is so acute, how can publicly funded broadcasters and internet intermediaries be persuaded to compete fairly?

She offers some important principles on which future regulation and legislation may be based.

THE EUROPEAN UNION: In 2010 is Copyright still able to protect and reward the creative heart of Europe?

Imagine you are reading this page back in 1990. This morning you pored over your favourite newspaper, folded it and put it down to finish later.

Or in 2000? That same title seemed a bit slimmer today. And was it a touch brasher? You had looked on its website yesterday and wondered for a moment how you would feel if that relatively succinct set of electronic pages which you browsed somewhat awkwardly (not really used to the online game) became the norm. Surely paper papers were immortal?

Now in 2010, you have just read your famous broadsheet which you know has a rapidly falling readership and wondered whether its online doppelganger really will supersede paper – perhaps via a handheld device? A different physical and intellectual experience. You know that worldwide some great newspaper titles are on the brink, facing tumbling advertising revenues and increased competition – from free dailies, internet intermediaries, multiple TV and radio sources, some of which continue to be state funded! And in print at least a steadily declining readership, especially among young people who often skim news from bookmarked blogs or search engines which throw up headlines, brief descriptions, unconfirmed sources, facts and fictions.

Jump to 2020, in each major EU market two or three of the major titles have folded for ever. One or two have retained a pale memory of their vivid parentage. Most news is online now that TV and press have effectively migrated and merged. The great majority of folk get their video news clips from websites or what used to be TV Channels. Whatever happened to analysis and investigative journalism?

What went wrong? How did we let it happen? Who was to blame? Much more important what action are we taking right now to try and avoid that alarming future?

Back to 2010 when let's face it, our total audience has never been greater thanks to all the outlets now available.. Audience is not our problem. Getting paid for our content is. Without proper protection for our intellectual property, and innovative ways to licence and manage our content, any future investment in news media through trusted brands appears unsustainable.

So the question facing us today is how do we safeguard copyright on the planet of the internet to help preserve not only newspapers and professional journalism but creative production across all the media? How do we stop – some say – the loggers cutting down the rainforests of creative content that once were home to news, comment and artistic expression…in music, in video, in print and on the airwaves? But that of course is the global problem. What about our own more temperate landscape of Europe?

Within the Single Market framework, the European Union has been harmonising copyright legislation for over two decades. In April 2001 an EU Directive for online copyright was adopted to adapt copyright law to reflect the latest technological developments. This was part of the effort to encourage the development of an Information Society for the already ubiquitous internet.

In 2005 the idea of a European Digital Library was born and the Commission published a new Communication which included legal challenges to established copyright legislation. The launch of this digital "Europeana" led to several further Green Papers, Communications and Consultations about what to do about "creative content online", and was followed in 2009 by the Communication on copyright in the Knowledge Economy. The Commission aimed to tackle the challenges of mass-scale digitisation and the dissemination of copyrighted content by asking us to consider certain new exceptions to copyright especially when it is hard to identify who owns copyright works (so-called Orphan works). While many observers would acknowledge the role played by exceptions and limitations in maintaining the balance inherent in copyright law, a real danger loomed that sweeping or unbalanced exceptions would inhibit the rapidly growing market for creative content online. The incentive for creators and producers to develop new services would have been removed. Lively concern was expressed by many media voices.

The European Commission then issued a Reflection Document[1] towards the end of 2009 on the expanding digital universe and its effects on the media and creative businesses in Europe. They dealt with three key areas:

- Consumer access

- Commercial user access

- Protection of Rights-holders

In doing so they concentrated on the musical and film industries which have suffered profoundly from piracy over the last decade. Only once, in the opening paragraph, did the Document mention newspapers and magazines despite the crucial fact that any mandatory Law would have significant impact on the whole publishing industry. In dealing with Rights they made one startling omission: there was no discussion of Automated Rights Management which means adapting copyright to the technology and geography of the internet.

The Reflection Document raised vital questions for us to consider in 2010. The first must be: What policies should we pursue to develop a management system for copyright that is fit for the 21st century? Copyright is central to the answer but it must be founded upon a dynamic rights management infrastructure which enables everyone to have access to the European treasury of creative content.

Infrastructure here means the technical standards, the software, the databases and the services that make it easy for the user to find, access and use publishers' content across a range of devices from mobiles to TVs. But to do so in a way which respects the rights of the copyright holder and clearly accommodates any exceptions and limitations. This is absolutely essential to the future of not only a free press but a viable and profitable publishing industry as a whole.

So let us look more closely at what the Commission's Reflection Document proposed. It sought "an ambitious European Digital Agenda which should include targeted legislative action" with the

---

[1]   http://ec.europa.eu/avpolicy/docs/other_actions/col_2009/reflection_paper.pdf

aim of creating "a modern, pro-competitive, and consumer-friendly legal framework for a genuine Single Market for Creative Content Online", in particular by:

- "creating a favourable environment in the digital world for creators and rightholders, by ensuring appropriate remuneration for their creative works, as well as for a culturally diverse European market;"

- "encouraging the provision of attractive legal offers to consumers with transparent pricing and terms of use, thereby facilitating users' access to a wide range of content through digital networks anywhere and at any time;"

- "promoting a level playing field for new business models and innovative solutions for the distribution of creative content."

These may be laudable hopes for the Commission, for business and for consumers but not all such aims are necessarily compatible. To help address these objectives but also any intrinsic conflicts, the European Publishers Council has invited the Commission and all concerned to address six Principles and act to:

- Principle 1: cherish the fundamental role of copyright in providing the incentive to invest in the commercial production and dissemination of creative content.

- Principle 2: respect the entitlement of copyright holders to choose how their content is made available, accessed and used.

- Principle 3: promote freedom of choice in licensing solutions.

- Principle 4: make sure that the system of rights management carefully balances rights, exceptions and limitations.

- Principle 5: take a balanced approach to the challenge of digitising Europe's analogue print legacy.

- Principle 6: uphold the publishing industries' unique economic, cultural and social contributions to the changing digital Europe.

And how can the Commission, industry and consumers work together to achieve such essential aims which are critical to the prosperity of all the media and the very continued existence of some? And to do so not for a static market but for a world in which the one thing we can guarantee is continuing technological change!

Here is a Plan to consider:

1. Fair Competition: Recognise and promote investment by Europe's publishers by ensuring that, as rights-holders, they are in no less favourable a position – online than other producers and distributors of digital content.

2. Fight Piracy: combat all forms of *piracy* of copyright content and ensure full implementation of the EU Enforcement Directive.

3. Freedom of Choice: preserve publishers' freedom to choose licensing solutions. These must be designed to give business users and consumers access to products and services across digital platforms and devices while *respecting* the principle of authorised use.

4. Technical Solutions: encourage the development of technological solutions for rights management that are effective in law; recognise that technology is an *enabler* of rights management, *not* a replacement for copyright.

5. Digitising collections: Work with rights-holders to meet the challenge of digitisation of existing collections in libraries and archives in a *balanced* way and in accordance with *established* copyright principles of prior consent by right holders.

6. Orphan Works: develop a harmonised approach to Orphan Works, based on the need for a 'diligent search' proposed by the High Level Expert Group. Find collective management and technical solutions recognising that Orphan Works will thus become a diminishing issue.

7. Exceptional Solutions: resist the extension of mandatory exceptions to copyright unless there is a proven case that the existence of different *national* exceptions constitutes a real barrier. The Commission should encourage broad collaboration to ensure that existing exceptions and limitations are accommodated within licensing solutions and encourage the development of *automated* methods of facilitating exceptions.

8. Adaptive Innovation: apply a test of 'adaptive innovation' to the development of the copyright framework. Adapt existing solutions for copyright because they have a long-proven track record of economic and cultural success. Avoid the introduction of inappropriate or untested measures which could damage well-established creative businesses.

In the last decade, new technological developments have made the enforcement of copyright more necessary than ever. Peoples' perceptions have changed. It is now a common misconception that the "free and open Internet" is the place to go for a free lunch. This has led to unprecedented levels of piracy, even on a business to business level where some companies profit from content that somebody else has struggled to create. The "free flow of information" does not mean products and content available for free. It means access to a vast universe of information and, may be, knowledge but not necessarily at no cost.

But how could one cut down on piracy and reduce the unauthorised taking or theft of content? One Adaptive Innovation has been the project to establish a mechanism to help manage those endangered rainforests of content. It goes under the acronym of A.C.A.P. meaning Automated Content Access Protocol.[2] ACAP aims to stop illegal logging. It cannot stop entry to the forest nor indeed, if the entrant is determined to ignore the law, the taking of logs. But it can and does put up warning © notices at every entry point, notices that are legible not only to human loggers but to the robots and crawling mechanisms that scan, index and copy great chunks of the web in less than the twinkling of a human eye. Those notices (with equal velocity!) say "This is my land and yes the timber may be for sale but please do not steal it, please ask permission before you enter and help yourself to my logs".

More than 1900 websites in over 57 countries have already installed and use this protocol of serving prior © notice on uninvited visitors or commercial predators. However the major Search Engines have so far chosen not to teach their crawlers to read the ACAP language. Their motives appear mixed but copyright holders everywhere must actively seek the support of Government to hasten the adoption of ACAP as the vital method to safeguard copyright material by giving online © notice of permission to every digital machine which wants to enter.

As one sets out an argument for the future it is sometimes prudent to review the past to avoid proposing self serving mechanisms or mere commercial interest.

Remember how we got here?

Three hundred years ago, in 1709[3] the English Queen Anne gave her name to an:

---

[2] www.the-acap.org

[3] The 1709 Statute of Anne, "An Act for the Encouragement of Learning by vesting the Copies of Printed Books in the Authors or purchasers of such Copies, during the Times therein mentioned", took effect on 10 April 1710.

"Act for the Encouragement of Learning by Vesting the Copies of Printed Books in the Authors or Purchasers of Such Copies ... Whereas Printers Booksellers and Other Persons have of late frequently taken the Liberty of Printing, Reprinting and Publishing or causing to be Printed, Reprinted and Published such books or other Writings without the consent of the Authors or Proprietors of such books and writings to their very great detriment and too often to the Ruin of them and their Families..."

In 1777, Beaumarchais founded the first French Society of Authors to promote the recognition of the rights of authors to profit from their Works. In the 1780s, Noah Webster was anxious to protect his rights in The American Spelling Book ...

These are crucial rights not mere commercial properties. Men and women who produce creative work need the incentive to write or report or comment. There may be an intellectual or moral or spiritual reward but they cannot live by bread alone. They need financial reward too. So protection and promotion of their rights is essential in any civilised society. Indeed in order to emphasise just how crucial Intellectual Property Rights are, more than 300 publishers from all over the world have signed the Hamburg Declaration which opened for signature in 2009. It declares: "...universal access to publishers' services should be available but... we no longer wish to be forced to give away our property without having granted permission".[4]

In a world that is experiencing the greatest, fastest technological changes ever, let no man impose unwise or damaging or, worse perhaps, just easy solutions on that part of the creative world which feeds not only our minds but helps build our homes, cook our food, print our books and shape our very society. Free creative dialogue is a corner stone of the whole edifice. We must keep it safe.

---

[4] http://www.epceurope.org/issues/Hamburg_Declaration_on_Intellectual_Property_Rights.pdf

Happy Birthday to Copyright

SIMON JUDEN

CHIEF EXECUTIVE, PUBLISHERS ASSOCIATION

Simon Juden submitted this article as Chief Executive of the Publishers Association, a position he held from May 2007 until 2010 when he moved to Pearson to become head of public policy.

Simon Juden was born and brought up in Norfolk and read Pure Mathematics at Emmanuel College, Cambridge, going on to complete a PhD at the University of Bath. He taught at Eötvös Loránd University in Budapest before working with satellites as a scientist and computer programmer. He went freelance in 1997, first as an IT expert and later as a management consultant, working on a variety of programmes within the high technology sector for companies like Vodafone, Data General, Proquest and Manugistics.

He joined the board of the Professional Contractors Group (a trade body for freelance workers) in 2001, becoming its full-time chairman in 2004. He left to join the Publishers Association as CEO in May 2007. The production and consumption of digital product is a particular interest of his, and he speaks and writes on publishing in a digital age in a variety of fora within the UK and Europe.

Abstract: The UK's economy used to be predicated on manufacturing. Then it was predicated on services, in particular financial services. Now and going forward, most commentators agree that the Knowledge Economy is of critical and central importance to the UK. The publishing industry is the lifeblood of that Knowledge Economy, not only through the dissemination of knowledge but also indirectly through support of the academic infrastructure as well as driving social change and social mobility. All of that value – and indeed 8% of UK Plc – is predicated on copyright.

Technology is blurring boundaries between what have hitherto felt like very different businesses and sets of rights. New business models are emerging and new players are bringing disruptive changes to the marketplace. Copyright has always evolved to meet changing realities and no-one can be in any doubt that further evolution to fit tomorrow's markets will – indeed, must – follow.

At its heart, copyright gives creators ownership of their work and investors confidence that they will realise a return if what they risk money on works well. These two core principles must remain sacrosanct if the UK is to continue creating (and exporting) the high value content so valuable in social, scientific, cultural, educational and economic terms.

Happy Birthday to Copyright

Copyright is the essential legal protection for authors, publishers and other creators in the world of literary and related works in the United Kingdom (where it was given statutory form for the first time 300 years ago, in the 1709[1] Statute of Anne). It has grown from this beginning to form the main legal basis for the worldwide publishing industry, which contributes so much to literature, learning and culture not only in the UK but in every country and every language in the world. The most recent government figures estimated that the UK creative industries alone comprise 8% of the UK's economy, the largest part of which comes from publishing. This does not include the additional income created by original works based on books, such as films, radio and TV programmes, which must contribute even more, even in the UK, and it does not begin to estimate the benefits which have accrued globally, and which copyright protects.

The Knowledge Economy is of critical importance to the country's future. Publishing is front and centre in delivering the opportunities it affords, both directly through the dissemination of knowledge and indirectly through support of the academic infrastructure, as well as driving social change and social mobility through literacy.That contribution is predicated in a fundamental way on copyright, and in particular the ability to make a return on creative and financial investment.

Copyright, of course, does not protect everything, but provides vital legal safeguards for original works that have been developed into a permanent form by the investment of time, skill, and money by the creator, be that an author or a publisher. The literature which results is a culturally significant product of inestimable value. Society rightly expects reasonable access to the work, both after the term

---

[1]   The 1709 Statute of Anne, "An Act for the Encouragement of Learning by vesting the Copies of Printed Books in the Authors or purchasers of such Copies, during the Times therein mentioned", took effect on 10 April 1710.

of copyright has expired, and during it, by means of agreed exceptions such as that for research and private study. So the creator's, or creators', exclusive rights of copyright are balanced by a limited term of years and by copyright exceptions for users such as libraries and educational establishments wishing to have access in the public interest. The resulting formula, even after 300 years, is a balanced system which works not only for authors and publishers, but is in the public interest too. So – many happy returns to UK copyright.

Being 300 doesn't mean being obsolete or outdated

The story of copyright since 1710 has been one of almost constant revision to accommodate new formats, works and technologies, such as sound recordings, films, TV programmes, computers and now the internet. This process of continual development is in all our interests, both as rights-holders, users and society as a whole, and ensures that the framework keeps pace with the accelerating changes in technology, while maintaining the vital balance of interest outlined above. Amongst recent examples we can number the World Intellectual Property Office (WIPO) Copyright Treaty of 1996, giving specific protection to Technical Protection Measures, and Digital Rights Management metadata, together with a new "making available" right, balanced with continuing discussions about exceptions for users with special needs, such as visually impaired people. The 1996 Treaty was implemented throughout the EU following the 2001 Copyright Directive, which was implemented in the UK via 2003 Regulations. So a great deal of our copyright law is only 7 years old, and all of it is subject to regular reassessment to gauge its relevance and usefulness. Compared with some legal systems, therefore, copyright is comparatively young, and in a state of constant renewal as new technologies and business models come to the fore.

Copyright is fundamentally fit for purpose in the 21st century

Even the comparatively recent developments outlined above were comprehensively reviewed by the government's Gowers Review, which reported in its 2006 Final Report that intellectual property law in the UK was as fit for purpose in the 21st century as it had ever been, although capable of further improvement through a number of specific revisions on detailed points. The Gowers recommendations are still being discussed in 2010 by the UK's IP Office, and it is likely that revised exceptions will be introduced soon for distance learning and format shifting for preservation and archiving – all proof that the framework can be readily adapted in the best interests of the digital economy without undermining the fundamental securities it provides.

Copyright and the Internet are not enemies

The internet is of course a major challenge to copyright, as it is to all territorially – based laws. Many feel the natural democracy and freedom of the internet should mean all content should be freely available to all around the world. However, this assumes an endless supply of new, original, authentic and reliable scientific and cultural content can be produced at no cost to anyone, a charming but naive proposition. Someone has to pay for original content, and free content is no more realistic than free beer. Apart from user-generated content like blogs and Wikipedia, most authentic, peer-reviewed content of any value needs significant investment, and that investment – of skill and expertise as much as money – needs protection; in the borderless era of the internet, that protection must be global. But there is no reason to suggest this means copyright and the internet should be enemies. On the contrary, the 300 year history of copyright shows that it can adapt to technology, and be strengthened by it, just as has been the case for every other breakthrough in the dissemination of works and ideas.

Rights-holders are users, too

Many of the challenges to copyright in the digital age are equally challenging for rights-holders; a useful counterbalance to fears of rights-holder "monopoly". A key difficulty for would-be users in obtaining permission to reproduce copyright works is what to do when you encounter an "orphan work", whose rights-holder cannot be located, even after a diligent search. This is a hurdle for rights-holders as well, as many publishers need to reproduce substantial portions of text or illustrations in the creation of anthologies or encyclopedias, and in doing so needs permission from other publishers, or picture galleries. Potential solutions have been discussed at UK, EU and international level amongst rights-holders, libraries and other users. This dialogue has been constructive, and both rights-holders and users are optimistic about the prospects of developing a universally agreeable solution, such as the creation of orphan works licences to be offered by rights-holder bodies. One likely solution may come from the current EU-sponsored ARROW project, which is in the process of building common rights and permissions systems based on interoperable metadata across all 27 member states of the EU – a project which will facilitate the digitisation and "unlocking" of our cultural heritage on a vast and unprecedented scale.

Copyright is about creativity as well as enforcement

No publishing industry can grow if creativity is not protected and encouraged, and enforcement is in the interests of all those who create and enjoy creative content. Despite national, international and digital piracy being a real problem for copyright owners, publishers' primary motivation is to publish as widely as possible, at a price which their readers can afford. In developing countries this may mean sponsoring a reduced price local edition, which represents considerable investment and risk for the UK and local publisher or agent, particularly if pirates get hold of the material, and local enforcement measures via the police or courts become necessary to protect the author's and publisher's work.

In the UK, publishers go to great lengths to avoid suing their own readers, despite the rise in digital piracy. In preference to pursuing legal action, the Publishers Association has recently launched a Copyright Infringement Portal, which has achieved great success in delivering simple, automated Notice and Takedown requests to people offering unauthorised or illegal downloads of copyright material. Recent surveys suggest success rates around 80%, since most people are not pirates or criminals, and would prefer instead to be legitimate users of our authors' work.

Copyright – The Future?

Technology is blurring boundaries between what have hitherto felt like very different businesses and sets of rights. New business models arc emerging and new players are bringing disruptive changes to the marketplace. Copyright has always evolved to meet changing realities and no-one can be in any doubt that further evolution to fit tomorrow's markets will follow. Indeed there are a number of such changes that we believe to be essential.

Copyright, if you strip it down, has at its core two principles. If you created it, it's yours. And if you invest in something that makes a return, that return belongs to you. Weakening either of those two core principles puts at risk not only the 8% of the economy currently predicated on copyright, as well as millions of attendant jobs; but also the often intangible value in social, scientific, educational and cultural terms that the creative industries deliver to the UK.

Copyright is the essential enabler for the digital economy. If proper standards and tools are implemented, consumers shouldn't need to understand copyright in order to use and enjoy content; and creators should be protected from the abuse of technology. Copyright represents a balance between the needs of everyone in the value chain: creators, businesses which invest at risk to bring content to audiences, and consumers. As we move ever further into the digital epoch, it is critical that that balance is preserved.

The internet today is a morass of mediocrity, punctuated by high value content. Some of that high-value content is "user-generated"; but much of it is not and never can be. No-one is going to take months or years crafting a work, or invest money in the continued creation of content, if the ability to make a return is compromised. Proper econometrics and a credible, rigorous evidence-base – which should not take too long to build – must underpin policy-making in this critical area.

The UK's future depends fundamentally on the further development of the Knowledge Economy. It surely follows that copyright must always work in ways which give authors and publishers the confidence both to take time creating high value works and to make them available. As business models and copyright continue to evolve, this is the principle to which we must hold fast.

The Answer to the Machine

MARK BIDE AND ALICIA WISE

Mark Bide

Mark Bide has worked in and around the publishing industry for nearly 40 years. In January 2009, he was appointed Executive Director of EDItEUR, the trade standards body for the global books and serials communities. He is also a Director of Rightscom, the specialist London-based media consultancy, where among other client engagements, he is the Project Director for the ACAP project, working to standardise protocols for the machine-to-machine communication of permissions in the network environment. Before he joined Rightscom in 2001, he ran his own consultancy business for nearly 10 years. His publishing career began at Pergamon Press in 1971. He went on to become a Director of the European subsidiaries of both CBS Publishing and John Wiley & Sons. He is a Visiting Professor of the University of the Arts London.

Alicia Wise

Alicia Wise submitted this article as Chief Executive of the Publishers Licensing Society (PLS) and Head of Digital Publishing to The Publishers Association (PA), a position she held until until June 2010. PLS is the not-for-profit organisation owned by ALPSP, the PA, and the PPA that oversees collective licensing arrangements for UK publishers. PLS distributes approximately £25m per annum in copyright royalties to publishers.

Alicia holds a Ph.D. in Anthropology from the University of North Carolina – Chapel Hill. Prior to joining the publishing industry she worked as an academic and archaeologist, then joined the Joint Information Systems Committee first to manage national negotiations for access to a broad array of intellectual property and then to direct research and development programmes to stimulate the innovative use of information technology in further and higher education. Alicia became Director of Universal Access at Elsevier in June 2010.

Abstract: As we move further into the 21st century, publishers should heed Charles Clark's timely advice that "the answer to the machine is in the machine". It is not copyright as law that is the problem. Rather we need to embrace technology not only as a publishing medium but as the way to manage copyright on the internet. There are a number of diverse projects pointing the way to this future but there is an urgent need to bring these together into a coherent rights management infrastructure to ensure the future of a vibrant and diverse copyright industry.

The Answer to the Machine

Introduction

As we enter the second decade of the 21st century, we do well to recall Charles Clark's aphorism "the answer to the machine is in the machine" – an observation which he first made more than fifteen years ago when the digital age was still in its infancy. The copyright industries have spent much of the intervening period largely ignoring his pithy advice.

The thesis is straightforward enough. Copyright as law is entirely fit for the new environment of networks and digital dissemination. But traditional practice for the management of copyright – individually lawyer-crafted licences, communication on paper, people-heavy processes – can only be a thing of the past.

We need to find ways of managing copyright that go with the grain of technology rather than falling back on cross-grained attempts to maintain a vanishing status quo. The internet inevitably brings with it the end of traditional ways of doing business, of high barriers to entry, of incumbency rights. Nevertheless, there is absolutely no compulsion on society to accept that "information wants to be free" or that copyright itself has somehow become an outmoded concept. There are many who would like it to be so – and some with strong commercial interests that it should be so. But before we allow them to destroy what copyright has created, we should think very hard about what we would be losing in its destruction.

Copyright was conceived as a tool to encourage creativity; over three centuries, it has become the engine of a hugely diverse media sector, a society which values the role of author and composer, of photographer and musician and recognises their right to decide. Without copyright (and related intellectual rights), the media as we know it today – whether in entertainment, education or the delivery of news or other factual information – simply could not and would not exist. The risks are obvious, as many of our media businesses seem in a long decline that can only end in one way.

There are those who believe that what we are describing are the death throws of the dinosaurs of old media and that other lither and more agile "internet savvy" businesses will arise to take their place in the content ecosystem. But there is precious little evidence to suggest that this is so – almost all the businesses that are making money out of content on the internet are dependent on other people's investment (of time and money) in creating that content. Platitudes about the value of "the link economy" count for nothing in the real world. Unless the individuals and businesses which create content can find a way of making a return on their investment, they will cease to create (and those with money to invest will put it elsewhere). Copyright is what makes it possible to make a return on creativity – and it is critical to the development of a thriving and diverse creative culture on the internet. Without copyright, society will be much the poorer. Currently, the diversity and richness of content on the internet is subsidised by content delivered in other – physical – distribution channels. When that subsidy is no longer available, or at least becomes much less significant – as must inevitably be the case – the internet will come to be a drab and uninteresting place. Unless we can re-establish the rule of law.

But how can we make copyright work in an environment where to make perfect copies and to republish content of any kind is so simple that we can all do it?

The answer to the machine must indeed lie in the machine. As we move into a machine-to-machine environment, the business of managing copyright must become a machine-mediated process, in which the complexity of copyright is completely hidden from the individual user, as it always has been in the past.

Technology builds very complex systems but, properly implemented, hides all that complexity from the user. You pick up your mobile phone when you are thousands of miles from home and dial the number of someone else's mobile phone who may be anywhere on the planet. And with little fuss or bother, and remarkably little delay, you are connected. And everyone gets paid for the call. As a user you don't need to understand how it happens – you just have to have confidence that it happens.

Why can't rights management work like that? The answer is, of course, that it could – but first we need to build the necessary technical infrastructure.

Building the 21st Century Rights Management Infrastructure

What would it mean to bring the management of copyright into the 21st century?

In the first place, we suggest that this isn't primarily about "digital rights management" – or at least not as this phrase is commonly understood. Technical protection methods (TPMs) may have their place in the management of copyright on the internet, but they lie at the end of a process of rights management, not at its beginning. Enforcement is not the first issue to tackle.

The primary issue is about using technology to do what technology is really good at – managing data, particularly managing well structured and standardised data, and using that data to automate the processes that control everything around us.

In the physical world, we have to identify the content – and we have become quite good at applying persistent identifiers to our products. Book publishing led the way with the introduction of the ISBN four decades ago, and demonstrated how technology could be used to automate and manage previously manual (and error-prone) commercial processes.

In the last decade, using metadata communication protocols (particularly ONIX), the industry has got much better at communicating the rich data that is needed to describe its products in a world where online retail now means that description is all we have to go on when we choose to buy something. But at least the thing that is being described is a tangible physical object with parameters that are relatively easily understood. The identification and description of physical products is simple in comparison with the requirement to manage the identification of the very intangible "content" – and even more so the description of rights permissions associated with the use of that content. For as content moves from the physical to the digital world, it becomes increasingly clear that the currency of commerce in content is not the content itself, but in the rights and permissions to access and use that content. Rights and permissions data moves centre stage.

Let us imagine a world where rights and permissions are managed automatically.

Alice wakes up and begins her day. As it's a Saturday there's quite a lot to do. First off is a videoconference with a board member in Australia to select a new supplier, next breakfast, then the change to watch her 7 year old son perform in a play. Alice then needs to cast her ballot in the local election, pay some bills, get the shopping in, chat with her Mum, and do a variety of other little tasks. How will she manage to squeeze it all in before dashing off to do volunteer work planting trees at the local forest trust? No worries. Her alarm clock is integrated with the household wifi, so from the moment she wakes up helpful reminders and planning tools are at her beck and call. While brushing her teeth the digital radio alerts her that it is almost time for that videoconference. She downloads the post on her way, and is delighted to see The Economist and The Times have arrived. She sits down and the videoconference begins with no hassle. Helpful the home wifi has compiled information about the tendering companies, and produced a risk analysis of each proposal. She's prompted to make a breakfast selection, and by the time the videoconference is ended the croissant is nicely warm and ready to devour. Her son's play starts up on Club Penguin, and is a great way for him to meet up with mates in London and Cape Town. Voting online takes a few minutes as does paying the council tax bill. Most of the other bills are set up already and only need a quick glance before they go off. The shopping is done through Ocado –it's reliable and the groceries will arrive on Tuesday morning. Mum still keeps a telephone which means Alice can't see her during their conversation but they are still able to chatter away. She hops in the car, and listens to some excellent 1990's Britpop along with a mix of more recent tunes inspired by the genre, as the GPS guides her to the planting site. So… what's happening? Well, there's a lot of sophisticated technological infrastructure, but the important point is that Alice can't see it. The family home has high-bandwidth wireless connectivity, and services are synched between home, car, work, and school. Each family member has a secure online identity which enables them to carry out very trusted transactions online and with minimal hassle. Attached to this identity is the entitlement to use online resources. The family pays a monthly subscription for access to what they want. No family member keeps a personal collection of music, videos, or texts any more – they simply access what's needed.The creators and publishers and distributors of all this content receive micropayments reflecting the usage of their material and their various contributions to its creation and dissemination. The content that is downloaded is recorded, and royalties allocated and automatically paid.

We need to be able to identify the content being used and who controls the rights in it; we need to be able to identify the user and the usage; we need to be able automatically to link these various entities together to complete a transaction. This is probably less complicated than connecting two mobile phones on opposite sides of the planet – but not a whole lot less complicated.

And whereas managing the metadata that enables us to sell books sometimes seems quite daunting, managing metadata for managing rights and permissions on this scale is of an altogether different order of magnitude. It requires that we hold in structured and codified form information that we have previously been content to keep on paper in filing cabinets – or in our heads.

This data (or at least those portions which do not threaten privacy or confidentiality) will need to be held in accessible registries (online databases) – and those registries linked together through a trusted (and trustworthy) messaging infrastructure. These in turn have links to secure transactional systems that handle payments potentially to support many different types of business model – from low value micropayments to high value "all you can eat" subscriptions. And this infrastructure has to be pervasive – as pervasive as the network itself.

A work in progress

In many different initiatives, coming from many different starting points, the work of building the infrastructure has already started. We do not have space here for a comprehensive tour d'horizon, far less for a detailed description of each of the projects, but the selection here points to the effort that is now being made by many different organisations to address this increasingly urgent challenge.

The DOI (Digital Object Identifier: www.doi.net) was established over a decade ago to provide a resolvable identifier infrastructure to manage intellectual property on the internet, and is finally beginning to make significant headway outside its "home territory", academic publishing. This is due to become an ISO standard in the near future. At the same time, ISO, itself has been working on two critical standards: the ISTC (International Standard Text Code: http://istc-international.org/) which enables the standard identification of textual works; and the ISNI (International Standard Name Identifier – still a work in progress) which should (inter alia) facilitate the creation of the appropriate link between content and rights-holder.

Structured approaches to expressing licences and permissions are exemplified by ONIX-PL (ONIX for Publication Licences: http://www.editeur.org/21/ONIX-PL/), a standard format for the communication of publishers' licences to libraries and other institutional customers) and ACAP (Automated Content Access Protocol: www. the-acap.org) a format for the communication of much simpler permissions expressions to manage online business-to-business transactions (including, for example, news aggregation). In the visual arts, we have the work of the PLUS Coalition (http://www.useplus. com/index.asp), an organisation which has made substantial progress in the development of standards to support the automated processing of the licensing of photographs and graphic arts. And, of course, there is the Creative Commons (http://creativecommons. org/), a philosophical movement as much as it is a standards initiative, which offers a range of machine-readable licences primarily appropriate to the management of non-commercial content. And at the more technical end, DECE (http://decellc.com/) is the most recent project to seek to deliver interoperable TPMs for home networks – for managing permissions in our growing consumer video and audio collections.

And we are also seeing the development of the first online rights registries, for example in the work of the Book Rights Registry (http:// www.googlebooksettlement.com/) being established in the wake of the Google Book Search preliminary settlement. In Europe, the ARROW project (http://www.arrow-net.eu/news/) has been established to facilitate the licensing of digitisation of library collections; this ambitious project has at its heart the concept of a distributed registry of rights information, linked by a "switchboard" – and we return to our telephone analogy. Other registries planned include a registry of photographic rights planned by the PLUS Coalition and possibly a European music rights registry.

Creative Convergence

It would be an entirely unjustifiable overstatement to claim that these diverse initiatives are all carefully fashioned parts of a well conceived master plan, and that each will simply slot into its allotted place. On the contrary, a key task of the next decade will undoubtedly be to pull these different initiatives together into a coherent functional infrastructure. No one of the projects holds the complete answer to the management of copyright on the network, but each has its own part to play.

In the meantime, every company in the creative industries needs to get its own house much more effectively in order. As the work to put together claims for the Book Rights Registry has demonstrated so clearly to book publishers, not knowing what rights you own and control has potentially serious consequences (and can involve enormous amounts of rather unproductive work). This may be understandable in dealing with the physical legacy, but cannot be excused in the management of today's digital inventory.

The building of this infrastructure will be a fitting tribute not only to the insight of Charles Clark, who died in 2006, but also to three centuries of copyright law.

Collective Licensing: Responding to the Challenges of the Digital Age

KEVIN FITZGERALD

CLA CHIEF EXECUTIVE

Kevin Fitzgerald is the Chief Executive of the Copyright Licensing Agency Ltd (CLA). He joined the CLA in 2007. During his tenure licence fee income has increased from £47m to £60m per year.

Kevin joined the Thomas Cook Group in 1997. Amongst his various roles he was one of the founders of thomascook.com, which grew to some £50m of turnover in just three years.

In 2002 he joined Pearson PLC as Managing Director of Rough Guides. He increased global sales by 50% and gross margin from 45% to 65% in four years. Kevin holds other public appointments/non executive directorships. He has an MA from Oxford University and is a Fellow of the Royal Geographical Society.

The future success of the UK economy is highly dependent on how intellectual property (IP) is managed both in the UK and globally. The digitisation of content brings both great advantages in terms of access but also threats in terms of a sustainable economic model for creators and publishers. In this article, Kevin Fitzgerald, the CEO of the UK's Copyright Licensing Agency and Chairman of the European Union group for Reprographic Rights Organisations, explores how collective licensing has been responsive to market demands with the inclusion of digital-born, Smartboard, Virtual Learning Environment and website content in its licences. He also observes the importance of working closely with UK government to ensure a robust international legal framework for IP. He works through the example of the UK education sector and concludes that collective licensing helps to balance the opportunities and threats of the digital age.

Collective Licensing: Responding to the Challenges of the Digital Age

Content digitisation, and the internet in particular, have changed the game for rights-holders and moved the goalposts for copyright, as the digital age continues to erode the traditional economic and legal models of our industry.

As we enter the 'teenies' decade we are getting used to living and working in an age where digital technology enables creative work and information to be published, shared and re-used more easily than ever. Our content is distributed via a myriad of organically evolving channels, many outwith professional publishers and authors. As publishers, libraries and bookshops have been relinquishing sole control of the distribution channels, information and creative content have become easier and cheaper than ever to make available and for users to access. This has made it harder for writers and other content creators to retain control over how their work is used. In this new world the relevance of copyright, and the wider protection of intellectual property (IP), rather than being rendered less significant, has, if anything, grown in importance. In fact the health of the UK's creative industries will increasingly rely on an effective system of IP protection; a fact recognised in the Gowers report to government:

> "The UK's comparative advantage in the changing global economy is increasingly likely to come through high value added, knowledge intensive goods and services. The Intellectual Property (IP) system provides an essential framework both to promote and protect the innovation and creativity of industry and artists".[1]

In the digital world, the ability to share content legally becomes ever more important.

As with the analogue world, all rights-holders still want their content to be used and they still want to be paid for their work. Licensing mechanisms are still part of the economic model, though they will have to evolve to remain relevant. And as secondary licensing through collecting societies helped to address market failures in the analogue world, so it can in the digital world. The Copyright Licensing Agency, CLA, is one such collecting society and exploring how it supports the education sector, just one of those which it serves, will demonstrate continued opportunities.

Experience from the education sector illustrates how CLA is responding to change and illustrates the advantages provided by the collective licensing model. The sector has been a key element of CLA's licensing income since the establishment of blanket licensing schemes for state schools and colleges in 1986 and higher education

---

[1]   Gowers Review of Intellectual Property, December 2006

in 1990. Our licences help over 11 million pupils and students to benefit from the permissions included.

In a digital environment, it is now more important than ever to understand what copyright material is used, how it is used and to obtain feedback from users. When the first education licences were issued in the 1980s, photocopying was the only common method of copying and print was the primary vehicle of delivery. The surveys we undertake across education for distribution purposes have shown that photocopying and printed distribution still remain important for education but also the growth in the use of material from more and more diverse digital sources. The prevalence of computers in schools has meant greater use of the internet in teaching. Widespread use of other media such as virtual learning environments (VLEs), interactive whiteboards and even mobile learning provide far more versatility in the ways in which content is delivered. At the same time, content is now often published digitally, with CDROMs, e-books and digital subscriptions playing an important role in education across the sector from primary schools to universities and adult education.

Modern education is therefore fragmented, diverse and complex. One of the key characteristics of the provision of learning in schools is the drawing together of teaching materials from a variety of sources, the personalising of them to adapt to students' needs and delivery in any number of discrete ways. For example, teachers will frequently generate their own lessons using material from electronic subscriptions and websites in addition to traditional textbooks. Then they will deliver their lesson via an interactive whiteboard, a mobile device or a virtual learning environment (VLE) network. There have been numerous encouragements from the UK government directing teachers to deliver this sort of 'blended learning'.

Whilst a digital learning environment offers huge benefits to students and teachers, it also presents new challenges regarding the management of copyright and obtaining of legal permissions.

CLA licences and the collective licensing system are uniquely placed to deliver a solution that balances properly the needs of all parties and realises benefits for the students, educational institutions, rights-holders and for society in general. Schools and universities avoid huge costs, financially, and in time and convenience by ensuring they have permissions in place without fear of infringing the rights of creators and publishers of content. They also have the best quality information and teaching materials available to them to teach students. In return, copyright payments are immensely important to publishers, since profit margins in specialist publications are thin and net revenue paid to publishers from copyright licensing goes directly to the bottom line. Writers and other creators receive money that enables them to make a living, or continue to create for the benefit of all.

Strong partnerships in education have allowed us to deliver key extensions to our licences over the past two years. In higher education, institutions can now extend their licence to include additional rights covering copying from digital sources such as e-books and e-journals. All CLA educational licences allow institutions and their teaching staff to utilise platforms such as VLEs and interactive whiteboards in their teaching. CLA is also working on solutions to facilitate 'networking' (the sharing of material between educational institutions via an intranet) – a development that is becoming more widely used in schools. A licence including the addition of free-to-view website content rights is also currently under development. This demonstrates that CLA's licence offering has had to evolve relatively quickly to incorporate new rights that meet the needs of users and also return secondary revenue to rights-holders for digital forms of copying and within a framework of legal permissions.

As can be seen from just one sectoral example the UK market often finds its own commercial solutions. Few creators or publishers are arguing for a heavy regulatory hand, however, the underlying legal infrastructure still needs to be fit for purpose. There have been a number of recent reports and consultations in the UK, including the Gowers Review, the Digital Britain Report and recent IPO consultations on the role of Copyright Tribunal and 'Developing a Copyright Agenda for the 21st Century', and others at the European Union and the UN's World Intellectual Property Organisation, WIPO. Relatively few of the recommendations contained in these various reports have yet been implemented.

CLA has made full submissions to these reviews and we have consistently reiterated our opinion that copyright is standing the test of time with the existing legislative framework still being fit for purpose. Important areas, such as enforcement and education need to be addressed and we are pleased that concrete proposals to deal with these issues have now emerged from the final Digital Britain report among others.

There have been fears recently at UN WIPO that some countries are seeking new exceptions to existing copyright conventions for the education sector in future international trade treaties. Thus far the British government has been robust in defending the interests of British publishers and creators as the UK educational publishing sector continues to generate significant foreign currency flows and supports the public diplomacy goals of the Foreign and Commonwealth Office in sharing British language and cultural values.

In summary, the needs of the market continue to change at an ever increasing pace. Creators, publishers, government and organisations such as CLA continue to respond to those changes. As Charles Darwin once said: It is not the strongest of the species that survives, nor the most intelligent, it is the one most capable of change.

Accentuate the Positive Aspects of Copyright for the Sake of Future Posterity

ANDREW YEATES

Andrew Yeates is a media lawyer and business affairs specialist whose career has included senior in-house roles within the television, film, music and publishing sectors since qualifying as a solicitor in 1981. Andrew served as Chairman of the DCMS led Creative Exports Group from 2003 to 2008 and is now a member of the UKTI Creative Industries Advisory Board.

He was appointed as a member of the DCMS Legal Deposit Advisory Panel in September 2005 and was reappointed for a second term of four years from 1 September 2008 to 31 August 2012 in August 2008. Andrew helped to set up The Educational Recording Agency in 1989 and served as Chairman from 1995 to 2004. Since then Andrew has continued working with the company as its General Counsel.

He has been Intellectual Property Adviser to PPA (Periodical Publishers Association) since 2004. Since April 2006 he has also worked as a consultant to Sheridans solicitors, dealing particularly on rights related issues for clients involved in film, television and online distribution, and as a consultant for British Equity Collecting Society. Andrew was appointed a Director of the British Copyright Council in September 2008.

Following qualifying as a solicitor Andrew joined Thames Television as Contracts Manager for Thames and its subsidiaries Thames Television International and Euston Films in 1981.

He left Thames in 1987 becoming Company Lawyer for Phonographic Performance Limited and then joining Channel 4 in 1988. He worked with Channel 4 in a number of roles during the next 11 years including as Head of Acquisitions and Business Affairs and finally for 4 years as Corporation Secretary and Head of Rights.

In 1999 he joined the BPI (the record industry trade association) initially as Director of Legal and Business Affairs and then as Director General of the BPI and a Director of Brit Awards Limited from 2000 to 2004.

Since leaving the BPI he has continued as a Governor and Director of the BRIT School.

Abstract: 300 years after implementation of The Statute of Anne, copyright is in the legislative spotlight at national, European Community and international levels with unprecedented intensity.

Andrew Yeates argues the importance of accentuating the positive aspects of copyright within the debate, for the sake of future posterity.

Copyright exists for all. It is not exclusive. It is a simple premise to recognise the value of original creative work. Balancing the public interest in access to learning with the importance of innovation and progress will remain as important in the digital age as the early age of the printed word.

Copyright is the key to this. It is a golden key that must not be melted down to the point where it is unable to unlock creativity for the future.

Accentuate the Positive Aspects of Copyright for the Sake of Future Posterity

On 10 April 1710, The Statute of Anne entered into force within Britain. The long title describes the legislation as "An Act for the Encouragement of Learning, by vesting the copies of Printed Books in the Authors or purchasers of such Copies, during the Times therein mentioned". Encouragement and learning: good positive pillars upon which to build part of the legal system which has become an increasingly important and relevant part of the lives of everyone.

300 years on, it is a challenge for creators and for government to ensure that the public as a whole understand why copyright is important, and how it helps to enrich the lives of all. We must accentuate the positive aspects of copyright for all.

From 1710, the British system for recognition of copyright was adopted throughout the British dominions and provided the basis for British participation in debates which have subsequently led to the adoption of international copyright treaties in countries around the globe.

Copyright has now supported and helped to promote and protect creativity and innovation for the last three centuries. Creative industries have been identified and promoted by Government as an increasingly significant economic and cultural success story.

At international level this economic significance has been acknowledged by the conclusion of the TRIPS Agreement[1] within the framework of the World Trade Organisation.

Within the United Kingdom, technological developments touch on the lives of ordinary people in increasingly diverse ways. The creative industries are often at the forefront of technological change. They encourage people to "try out" new technologies which support the entertainment, education and information developed and distributed by creators, artists and performers. This is one of the many reasons why the creative industries are increasingly acknowledged by Government as a vital part of the United Kingdom economy.

This recognition is summed up well within the Executive Summary of the paper © *the way ahead: A Copyright Strategy for the Digital Age 2009* published at the end of last year by the Intellectual Property Office and BIS (Department for Business Innovation and Skills). The paper states "The last 300 years have seen an unprecedented explosion in the cultural, scientific and historical material available to scholars, business people and private citizen. Financial and societal rewards to creators and investors have helped continue to fuel the engine of creativity. Copyright has been in the background of much of this activity."

Yet, despite this economic and cultural success, technology is being used by some to challenge the validity of copyright. Technology (particularly new forms of digital electronic communication) now enables people to access copyright works more easily and quickly than ever before. The possibility of easy access is far too often used as a reason for seeking to reduce, or "do away with", the exclusive rights of authors and creators in the name of "copyright reform".

Instead of looking at the positive ways in which copyright works are being licensed and the benefits of the entertainment, education and dissemination of information resulting from the hard work and investment of creative people; recognition for the source of this value to society is being replaced by claims of "rights" to use the work of others without regard to entitlement to reward.

---

[1] Agreement on trade-related aspects of Intellectual Property Rights 1994.

Recent debates over new systems to help address the damage caused to creators by unauthorised online file sharing of copies of works have thrown up claims that unauthorised users have somehow had their human rights abused if an owner of copyright takes steps to prevent unauthorised use of their work.

Those who profit from taking and using the works of others without consent shout that they are being "persecuted" if they receive notices explaining that their unauthorised use of films, sound recordings and other copyright work, is illegal.

As we start the fourth century after the Statute of Anne, steps must be taken to put such claims into genuinely creative perspective. There are many ways in which this can be done. Consider a few examples:-

To accentuate the positive aspects of copyright people must understand that copyright exists for all

Recently it has been suggested that, simply because many individuals who write blogs, exchange photographs that they have taken, pass on copies of music that they have adapted, and otherwise distribute original works that they have created, are primarily interested in communication to others, such "authors" do not need copyright.

Why not? Since when did every creative work proved to have value for others in the longer term realise such value at the moment of creation?

If a person chooses not to "assert" copyright in their work, what benefit results to creators as a whole if such work does not attract the rights that "professionally" developed work attracts?

Creating new barriers for a creator to establish "professional status" or "commercial intent" before being entitled to authorise use of rights in their work, based upon the principles of copyright, will not encourage creativity and innovation in the future.

Instead it will create a division within society that will ultimately make copyright more "exclusive" rather than copyright works being made more available through transparent licensing regimes.

User-created content may be playing a new role in the digital world. However it must be wrong to deprive the creators of such work with the freedom to choose whether or not to assign, waive or exercise the copyright that exists in new work.

Taking a positive approach, if all new work starts with the same rights, owners can make their own choices over how to deal with their rights.

The copyright framework must be able to distinguish the subsections of "the public" which might claim the benefits of copyright exceptions and limitations from "the public" who are potential "consumers" or licensed users of copyright works

It is vital that copyright exceptions remain exception and do not become "the norm". Limitations limit application of rights. They must not dictate their application.

It must be right that exceptions to rights should only apply in special cases:-

* which do not conflict with the normal exploitation of the work or the subject matter; and

* which do not unreasonably prejudice the legitimate interests of the rights-holder.

The three step test established by The Berne Convention, and subsequently recognised in other international treaties, is an effective flexible base against which to test the practical effect of exceptions linked to the use of new technologies.

If we abandon this test, we may abandon a basis for international consensus which has served us well for many years.

It is a myth that the underlying framework of copyright law is too complex

Obtaining copyright protection under the existing copyright system is very cheap and simple, with no barriers for anyone with creative skills. It is applicable regardless of knowledge and financial standing. Copyright in terms of its application to individual works is not complex. New original work attracts copyright. This is something which society as a whole should seek to protect.

It is true that complexity arises when composite works are developed and marketed. Complexity also exists in establishing a need for certainty and fairness when introducing legislative exceptions to copyright, to prevent disproportionate detriment to those having their property rights restricted.

However these complexities have been addressed, and accommodated over three centuries. New works have been recognised and embraced as sound recordings were developed, films were made, broadcasting hit the airwaves and digital electronic transmission systems became a reality.

Digital is not so different that you need to tear up the copyright rulebook

The law of copyright has proved itself to be flexible in accommodating new technology. However, many now claim that digital "is different" in a way that demands a new copyright regime, without any real evidence of market failure.

In reality, copyright licensing can and does support myriad uses of copyright works. Broad changes to the current finely balanced copyright regime could lead to a two tier system, whereby the reduced protection de facto applicable to digital use makes it less attractive than analogue or more traditional print use.

Cannot this be the right positive approach for a digital age?

Suggesting copyright should require registration as a condition for recognition is not compatible with promoting the creative industries and knowledge economy

Work is needed to improve the ways in which copyright can be administered practically, economically and transparently. However, the framework for recognition of copyright, and the original work of all creators provides choices that need to be preserved to support administrative developments.

If we act positively to promote respect and accessibility for the work of creators, there must be no doubt that copyright will continue to serve communities around the world well for the next century, and beyond.

Copyright's Balancing Act and the Role of the Library

MICHAEL HEANEY

EXECUTIVE SECRETARY, THE BODLEIAN LIBRARIES OF THE
UNIVERSITY OF OXFORD

Michael Heaney is Executive Secretary at the Bodleian Libraries in Oxford. He joined the Bodleian in 1970 to catalogue East European books, and has worked his way through a variety of roles including responsibility for library automation, statistics and management information, publishing, and the quasi-legal issues of copyright, data protection and freedom of information. He is CILIP's academic libraries representative on the committee of the Libraries and Archives Copyright Alliance and has lectured on copyright issues in libraries. He is also a member of the Governing Board of the International Federation of Library Associations, in his capacity as Chair of IFLA's Division IV, 'Support for the Profession'.

Abstract: The copyright acts and legal deposit provisions have played a significant role in the development of the Bodleian since 1610. Over time libraries have taken on the task of being benevolent custodians of copyright works, and the library privilege provisions of the copyright acts recognise this. Queen Anne's Statute dealt with both the intellectual property and its material expression. From the invention of printing until the twentieth century the determining factor in the relation between the two has been the investment required in the means of production. The balance between them and the public good has been the subject of debate ever since. Starting with the invention of new media, travelling via the photocopier and continuing, but not ending, with digital media and the internet, the economic realities underpinning the means of production have changed. Where does the economic balance now lie, and where do libraries stand in the equation?

Copyright's Balancing Act and the Role of the Library

In 1859 The Scottish Annual carried a short piece by Jessie Edmondston entitled 'The sea-girt home'. The Family Herald carried another piece by the same writer. 'Steen: a Shetland story' in its

1 October issue that year. These pieces are long-forgotten and copies survive only in a few of the major research libraries, mainly in Scotland; but the author went on to a prolific career as one of Shetland's most famous authors, Jessie Saxby, with over 150 publications.[1] What makes these two works special is that 151 years after publication they are still in copyright: they were published when Jessie Saxby was just seventeen, and she died at the age of 99 on 27 December 1940.

Despite her prominence, I have not been able to find any republication of Jessie Saxby's work since her death, apart from the republication in 1974 by Norwood Editions in the United States of her 1932 work *Shetland traditional lore*. There is clearly not a commercial market for her work – certainly not for those early stories – but they are all still locked up behind the copyright wall protecting her creative investment. One might ask, cui bono?

The history of copyright is complex and can – and does – fill entire books, but we are celebrating the tercentenary of the Statute of Anne which first codified the concepts. There are two distinct aspects to copyright, and both are represented in the 1710 Statute. The first is the creation of the work, and the second its dissemination. The Act itself was intended to regulate the latter, by providing protection for the trade in books. Before Gutenberg, copying was a Good Thing; printing revolutionised our capability to spread information but was a specialised technology requiring skill and considerable investment. The protection of the author's intellectual property inherent in the printed item was almost a by-product. Under Anne, the right to authorise printing starts with the author, implicitly by his/her ownership of the manuscript copy; it passes to the printer by signed agreement, and on the expiry of fourteen years the copy/copies are returned to the author, who then has another fourteen years during which he/she can assign the printing rights.

Queen Anne's Statute also enshrined in law the agreement made one hundred years before between Sir Thomas Bodley and the Stationers' Company, providing for the deposit of copies in the Bodleian and later in other major libraries – recognising the role of libraries as custodians of learning.

The distinction between the created work and its dissemination was the subject of protracted dispute once the initial terms of copy-

---

[1] J. Laughton Johnston, *Victorians 60 Degrees North: The Story of the Edmondstons and Saxbys of Shetland* (Lerwick: Shetland Times, 2007). I am grateful to Brian Smith, Shetland Museum & Archives, for this information.

right granted by the Statute began to expire. The question was not settled until 1774 when the unpublished work was deemed to have perpetual copyright but publication set the clock ticking.[2] This then was the bargain: 'for the encouragement of learning', as the Statute had it: authors were encouraged to create and printers and booksellers to disseminate works by the provision of a monopoly right, but this right was time-limited, so that once the author and printer/bookseller had been able to recoup their investment, the public could benefit. The investment required to disseminate has resulted in a committed and focused publishing profession, while the consumers have been diffuse and unorganised. It is not, therefore, surprising that over time the balance of the bargain has shifted in favour of the producers – greater protection for longer periods. It is noteworthy that almost the only move in the other direction – the abolition of the perpetual copyright for unpublished work – is something that by its nature does not effected the balance of commerce. So after a century and more of the Berne Convention, a succession of Copyright Acts, WIPO treaties, European Directives and other provisions, we now have a system in which copyright in a work subsists, in the main, for seventy years after the creator's death.

Besides the copyright in the work there are also the neighbouring rights, such as in publishing, the copyright in the typographical arrangement, lasting for 25 years in UK law; and in music, the right in the recording qua recording , lasting for 50 years from release. These are rights relating to the dissemination of the work not its creation. It may seem at first glance odd that a lot of the debate conducted by publishers about rights focuses not on the right in the publication – the 25-year right – but in the authorial copyright, usually lasting, as we have seen, well over a century. Of course the publishers are the parties in the chain who have the most capital investment and the greatest degree of organisation, giving them the will and the ability to act in concert. In some sectors (particularly scientific journal publishing) the publishers have acquired the author's copyright, or a licence to publish which gives them equivalent rights. But if we continue to observe the bargain which attempts to strike the balance between stimulating creation and providing public benefit, we must continue to assess where that balance lies.

The basic variables in the equation are the costs of production, reproduction and distribution (both authorised and unauthorised).

---

[2]   William Cobbett, *The Parliamentary History of England* (London; Longman &c., 1806-1820), 17 (1813), cc. 1077-1110.

The lower the costs of production and authorised reproduction/distribution, the quicker the producer recoups the investment and makes a profit. If the costs of unauthorised reproduction fall, this will eat into the producer's profit. Digital technology over the past two decades has dramatically decreased all these costs. The focus so far has been on the upheavals experienced by the music industry, but there are analogous debates in other areas. Consumers have a habit of rebelling against what they see as unfair or rapacious practices, voicing such views as 'if record companies sold recordings at a fair price there wouldn't be so much unauthorised copying'. It is not even the first time it has happened – the nineteenth century saw major music piracy wars, with many of the same arguments – when new methods of printing sheet music enabled pirate printers to undercut mainstream music publishers. The mainstream publishers finally won legislative support just as the entire economic model was swept away by the invention of the gramophone.[3]

Rufus Pollock, an affiliate of the Cambridge Centre for Intellectual Property and Information Law, recently published an econometric analysis attempting to quantify the various factors so as to arrive at an optimal term for copyright protection.[4] Similar calculations underlay the CIPIL report to the Gowers review on the economic evidence relating to (and advising against) an extension of the term of copyright in sound recordings.[5] Pollock notes that as costs fall the need for extended protection diminishes; and that the greater the number of works in existence, the smaller the value of each one. The economic protection which each work requires should fall as a result. His primary conclusion is that the optimal term for copyright protection now is fifteen years. By calculating the results for a range of values for the variables he produces a graph showing the probability density function for these ranges.[6] This gives a 99th percentile value of 39 years – that is, for all reasonable values of the parameters in the equation, the result will be an optimal term of 39 years or less in 99 cases out of a hundred. This is not an unreasonable result – if the value of a work were to last for its entire term of

3   Isabella Alexander, 'Criminalising Copyright: A Story of Pirates, Publishers and Pieces of Eight', *Cambridge Law Journal*, 66.3 (2007), 625-656.
4   Rufus Pollock, 'Forever Minus a Day? Some Theory and Empirics of Optimal Copyright' http://www.rufuspollock.org/economics/papers/optimal_copyright.pdf.
5   http://webarchive.nationalarchives.gov.uk/+/http://www.hm-treasury.gov.uk/d/gowers_cipilreport.pdf.
6   Pollock, p.27.

protection, then Global Books in Print would have a very different character from that which we find. Publishers make decisions on publication based on a return on investment of just a few years, not on a return over the copyright term. The term of protection for a patent –even one that requires multimillion-pound investment – is just 20 years. The 25-year typographical copyright which protects the publishers' real investment is probably about right. If I were to visit my bank manager with an idea for a marvellous product which, however, needed over a hundred years –or even fifty – for me to build a sustainable business model and recoup my investment, I would very quickly be shown the door.

So for all practical purposes of the pursuit of commercial success, the term of copyright protection is absurdly long. Macaulay characterised it well in a debate about the extension of the copyright term in 1841:

Dr. Johnson died fifty-six years ago. If the law were what my hon. and learned Friend wishes to make it, somebody would now have the monopoly of Dr. Johnson's works. Who that somebody would be, it is impossible to say, but we may venture to guess. I guess, then, that it would have been some bookseller, who was the assign of another bookseller, who was the grandson of a third bookseller, who had bought the copyright from Black Frank, the Doctor's servant, in 1785 or 1786. Now, would the knowledge, that this copyright would exist in 1841, have been a source of gratification to Johnson? Would it have stimulated his exertions? Would it have once drawn him out of his bed before noon? Would it have once cheered him under a fit of the spleen? Would it have induced him to give us one more allegory, one more life of a poet, one more imitation of Juvenal? I firmly believe not.[7]

And this is only the world of works which have been through the commercial life cycle. Because publishing is now so easy that anyone can do it, many works are now published for reasons other than commercial gain. Even in the highly commercial world of scholarly journal publishing, the drivers of publication for authors are not direct commercial return, but the indirect rewards of peer esteem and career progression. Hardly any of these authors make arrangements to ensure that their intellectual property is conserved and actively managed throughout their lives and beyond. But they

---

[7]   Hansard, House of Commons Debates, 5 February 1841, vol 56, cc341-60 (http://hansard.millbanksystems.com/commons/1841/feb/05/copyright   accessed 17 February 2010).

are all protected by the automatic bestowal of copyright for two life-times.

I am not going to argue for a reduction in the copyright term – that will not happen – but this does have some consequences for libraries. Long after the books have been remaindered by publishers, forgotten by the reading public, and in many cases forgotten even by their owners, you will find them on the shelves of the great national, academic and municipal libraries. The orphan works problem is already well known, but the issues are even more complex. Libraries hold works which are commercially 'alive'; works whose copyright ownership is fully known but which are out of print and unlikely to be republished; works whose copyright ownership is known but unlocated; works known to be in copyright but whose current owner is unknown; works of uncertain copyright status; and out of copyright works. Libraries are honest and careful custodians of copyright and so they cannot make use of modern technologies to increase the availability of these works or even to meet the normal and reasonable expectations of users. A particularly poignant example is the grandchild of a South African author who after a long search had traced a copy of his grandfather's work published in the 1950s to one of our libraries in Oxford and wanted us to supply a copy. We had to point out that although in all probability he was, by line of descent, one of the owners of the copyright in the work, he was probably not the sole heir, and that in the absence of evidence about his ownership and rights we would have to decline his request. Cui bono?

Macaulay was right in principle but wrong in one respect. No one would have lost track of Samuel Johnson's intellectual property rights, and we can be sure that the works of J.K. Rowling and Winston Churchill will never become orphans. Where there's an economic interest it will be nurtured.

The dual thrust of Queen Anne's Statute – recognition of intellectual creations as property capable of being owned, and regulation of the trade in copies of that property – has, in its great-great-grandchildren, produced an active, creative and dynamic head in the publishing industry, which drags behind it a century-long tail of orphan and moribund works of which libraries are the primary custodians but upon which they cannot exercise their own considerable ingenuity for public benefit. But we can't blame Queen Anne for that; the evidence is that she got the term about right. So let's hear it for Queen Anne!

Copyright through the Looking-glass

TOM RIVERS

COPYRIGHT AND MEDIA CONSULTANT

Tom Rivers has worked for the last fifteen years as a copyright and media consultant. His clients have included BBC Worldwide and the Association of Commercial Television in Europe. He has also contributed to a European Commission research project on the value of the public domain and has worked for the US Agency for International Development in Bosnia Herzogovina. He joined the BBC's Legal Division in 1981 and was the Corporation's Head of Copyright from 1990 to 1995. Before qualifying as a solicitor he worked in book publishing in London and New York and ran a small publishing company in Cambridge, Rivers Press.

Abstract: Developments in computer and communications technology have put into the hands of ordinary people the means to join in a global interchange of information, ideas and forms of expression.

The problem of piracy in the digital environment can be addressed to some extent by technological means. Governments in western Europe have also taken legislative initiatives to impose some obligations on access providers.

Enforcement is made problematic because piracy is multi-territorial and therefore needs multilateral solutions. Developing countries are pursuing a different agenda at WIPO which is more focussed on exceptions and limitations than on updating rights or enforcement.

New business models squeeze the share going to rights-owners in the value chain.

The ideological issues relate to the control exercised by state and other authorities over the publication of dissenting material. There is a tension, reflected in the US law, between free speech and the Copyright Clause.

Large countries are likely to want to continue to provide protection for the intellectual productions of their own citizens.

Copyright through the Looking-glass

"Now, *here*, you see, it takes all the running you can do, to keep in the same place. If you want to get somewhere else, you must run at least twice as fast as that!" Lewis Carroll, *Through the Looking-glass*, ch. 2[1]

It may be hard to specify when the digital age began. But it is worth picking out some of the landmarks to help us see what it is that we are looking at.

A pebble at the top of the mountain: a prediction by Gordon E Moore, a co-founder of Intel.

In a paper published in 1965 Moore predicted that the number of transistors that could be accommodated at minimum cost on an integrated circuit would double every year. Subsequently, he adjusted the prediction to a doubling about every two years, and in that form it is now known as Moore's Law and has proved stunningly accurate.

In practical terms Moore's Law has meant that whereas the equipment comprising Manchester Mark I, the earliest full-scale implementation of a Turing machine, occupied three walls of a large lab at Manchester University in 1948, a consumer can now buy a laptop costing under £500. The distribution of computing power in consumer devices is a fundamental element of the digital age.

Conway and Mary Berners-Lee met while working at Ferranti on the first industrial version of Manchester Mark 1. Their son, Tim, born in 1954, is acknowledged to have brought the World Wide Web into existence in the early nineties – another landmark in the digital age.

According to UNCTAD mobile phone subscriptions in the continent of Africa grew from 54 million in 2003 to almost 350 million by 2008; in South Africa mobile phone subscriptions were equal to 1 per person; in Kenya the figure was 40 subscriptions per 100 inhabitants. The China Economic Review reports mobile phone penetration in China at 52.5% in the first half of 2009: this is roughly 670 million subscribers.

The picture then looks like this: we have a world which is more and more interconnected, and in which telecommunications, the internet and computer technology are putting more and more means

---

[1]   *Alice in Wonderland and Through the Looking Glass*, Collins Classics edition 1964, Page 164.

of communicating into the hands of ordinary people. Is this something we should welcome? Is it something we should be afraid of?

Whatever our hopes or fears it is clear we cannot turn the clock back.

And what has any of this to do with copyright?

For some stakeholders there is a very straightforward answer: piracy. It is now much easier, they say, to steal content, and much more difficult to catch the thieves. One answer is to find bigger and better locks to put on the doors. Another is to persuade the distributors (the people who own the pipes and the portals) to enlist in the fight against unauthorised users.

In France and in the UK legislation is now on the statute book which places some responsibility on access providers for what their customers do.

But in a global economy, enforcement becomes a political issue. Legislation if it is to be effective needs to have a multi-national reach. Many in the developing world see the TRIPS Agreement of 1994, which does provide for the possibility of trade sanctions, as a great concession which they made and which entitles them to pay back. The debate in the World Intellectual Property Organisation has consequently turned away from a normative agenda, which seeks to modernise rights, to a development agenda, which takes up once again the Stockholm Protocol concerns – in other words, ways to carve out exceptions and limitations to exclusive rights. Rather similar dynamics are at work in discussions at WIPO on patents and on traditional medicine.

Other aspects are at least as important as the political.

In the old world, copyright was about authorship, ownership and market control. In the new world, authorship and ownership survive, but market control is contested. The business models which are being adopted by the owners of the new means of distribution provide for thinner slices of the cake for content. What this means is that more of the consumer spend is going on new equipment, leaving less for copyright products, which are in any case increasingly being bundled with the equipment. This might turn out to be a less material consideration for what in the old world would have been thought of as print-based products, because in a digital world some of the old costs have evaporated as the print product goes digital – no warehouses, no paper. But the film industry, for example, has long lead times for product development and requires considerable front-end investment. It is also uncertain whether on-line distribution can replace theatrical distribution.

There are on top the ideological issues – "wars of religion" we may call them.

Before market control there were other forms of control. The ruler always had an interest in orthodoxy, as did the Established Church. The Index, the Inquisition, Star Chamber, Licensing and Stamp Acts are all manifestations of the same purpose.

The system of licensing operated by the Stationers' Company up until the legislation lapsed in 1681 gave the Company a monopoly of officially sanctioned publication. What was officially sanctioned by no means captures the entirety of what was available.

For instance, the thriving business of reporting parliamentary proceedings – not only not officially sanctioned but unlawful – involved the production of newsletters by scribes (no print) and more or less clandestine circulation to subscribers. Dissent, in the sense of religious and political opposition, was carried on in pamphlets, which were often scurrilous as well as anti-establishment. Gentlemen had copies of their poetry made to give (not sell) to their friends.

The Act of Anne does not seem to have made a great deal of difference in the short run to the practice of the established trade. It was other factors than copyright which were more influential. These included the rise in the level of literacy, the creation of a middling class of merchants and traders, and the emergence of a new literary form, the novel.

Meanwhile, traffic of the non-respectable kind continued to thrive: Tom Paine's Common Sense which argued the case for independence for the American colonies was published in Philadelphia in 1776 and sold half a million copies in the first year – Paine donating his royalties to Washington's Continental Army.

It is easy enough to see the potential tension which existed from the start in the US between, on the one hand, the power conferred on Congress by the Constitution "(t)o promote the Progress of Science and the useful Arts, by securing for limited Times to Authors and Inventors the exclusive Right to their respective Writings and Discoveries" and, on the other hand, the First Amendment bar on Congress making any law abridging the freedom of speech or of the press.

Dissidents, when they put their case to the public, have always made the claim that their speech is "free" in the sense that it is unconstrained, uncompromised by corrupt influence, but also not a product of the market. Hence the "free" press (which in fact later simply meant advertiser-supported), the samizdat movement, the anti-establishment press (Iskra, Claud Cockburn's The Week, I F Stone's Weekly, Private Eye).

Some of the denizens of the blogosphere would perhaps claim these as ancestors.

Will copyright survive?

The cynic's answer to that question is that efficient market regulation is indispensable within the borders of large geo-political entities. If this is true, then one would expect that the next 25 years will see countries like India, China and Brazil with fully developed systems for rewarding the intellectual productions of their own citizens.

The Changing Role of Copyright

ROGER PARRY

Roger Parry is Chairman of Future plc (consumer media), Media Square plc (marketing communications), Mobile Streams plc (mobile media) and YouGov plc (market research).

He was CEO of More Group plc and CEO of Clear Channel International. He was a founder and Deputy Chairman of Clear Media in China. He was a founder of Internet Indirect plc, a director of New Media Spark plc and of iTouch plc. He was Chairman of Johnston Press plc from 2001 to 2009. He is Chairman of Shakespeare's Globe Trust.

Roger was a journalist with BBC and ITV, and a consultant with McKinsey & Co.

Roger was educated at the universities of Oxford and Bristol. He is the author of three books and is a Visiting Fellow of Oxford University. Roger is 56. Married, one son. He lives in London and Hampshire.

Abstract: Copyright Laws have evolved over time to reflect changes in technology and social attitudes. They were not needed before the widespread use of mechanical printing. The legal power of copyright started in 1710 with the objective of "the encouragement of learning". Before copyright the protection of authors was based in the high cost of making copies. Shakespeare never published the full text of his plays in his lifetime to protect his income. When copyright has been ignored authors like Charles Dickens and Mark Twain were forced to rely on paid speaking tours to make money in countries where their works were printed without permission. The extension of the protection of intellectual property to music, film and television has been slow and complex. The development of digital media and the Web now needs a new legal regime without which there is a threat to the continued development of the creative arts.

The Changing Role of Copyright

This is an extract from a forthcoming book by Roger Parry to be called *The Ascent of Media* and to be published in 2011. It provides a very brief overview of the development of copyright.

***

The nature of copyright has changed over the ages to reflect new technologies, new media types and new social attitudes. The past gives insights into the way a revised legal regime might develop to reflect the realities of control intellectual property in a time of digital media.

Before mechanical printing, that is before Gutenberg in the 1440's, copyright was not a concept recognised or requested by authors. The costs of making copies of books by hand were very high, literacy very low and the number of copies made, therefore, very small. Most of the texts were classic religious or scientific issues. The value created went to the books "manufacturer" – the scribe or the monastery – rather than the original author who was often not an identifiable individual in any event.

Before printing was invented contemporary writers made their living in other ways. Chaucer, for example in the late 1300's, wrote because he could afford to and he enjoyed Royal patronage. Edward III granted him "a gallon of wine a day, for life". He probably controlled the making of the initial copies of his books himself so that he could enjoy some literary income from the limited sales.

At the time that William Shakespeare was writing his plays, around 1600, there was still no legal way for an author to own the copyright on his work although mechanical printing was well established. One reason he never published the text of his plays in his lifetime was that he made his money from the tickets at live performances. To keep their work propriety he, and most of his contemporaries, only provided their actors with the scripts of their own characters. The entirety of the play's text remained with the writer to make unauthorized performance and publishing the full text more difficult.

The idea of patents over inventions of machines and techniques had been around since the 1400's when the Republic of Venice recognised various glass-making methods as being "patent" and thus restricted their use to certain approved artisans. But the notion of being able to control an idea or to own intellectual property or a story was not familiar in the Middle Ages. It was a source of frustration to authors and playwrights that any printer rather than the writers themselves benefited from the sale of copies their work.

The scarcity and the value in a printed document was protected by the relatively high cost of making it and by the fact that, in England, the Crown had granted monopoly rights to members of The Stationers' Company. They were the only ones who could legally, operate printing machinery. The Stationers enjoyed a form of copyright as all printed work had to be lodged with them in their library. The only mass media of the time was, thus, controlled by them by virtue of their printing monopoly rather than a legal framework over intellectual property.

But as science and industry evolved specialist writers wanted a way to retain the value of their own ideas. They lobbied for a solution and Queen Anne obliged. In 1710 the British Parliament enacted the so-called Statute of Anne – at the time the term "copyright" was not in use. The Statute was subtitled:

"An Act for the Encouragement of Learning, by vesting the Copies of Printed Books in the Authors"

It went on to give the rationale as

"Whereas Printers, Booksellers, and other Persons, have of late frequently taken the Liberty of Printing, Reprinting, and Publishing Books and Writings without the Consent of the Authors (of such Books and Writings) to their very great Detriment, and too often to the Ruin of them and their Families: For Preventing therefore such Practices for the future… [we propose this Act]

The idea was that to encourage writers to share knowledge and produce entertainment they must be allowed to obtain an income no matter who chose to publish their work. They, the writer, would own the copyright (not the printer) and it would stay with them for 14 years. At the time it was a radical idea but it proved very successful and paved the way for the professions of author and journalist and greatly helped the development of the novel as an art form.

It is probably no co-coincidence that what is regarded as the first English language commercial novel Robinson Crusoe by journalist Daniel Defoe was written just a few years after copyright protection was accepted and it proved the forerunner of many other works of fiction. It was this huge increase in books that led a group publishers to commission Dr Johnson to write his famous dictionary for which he was paid the handsome fee of 1,500 guineas to hand over his copyright to the consortium – an early example of an advance.

Initially the American colonies adopted the same rules but after their revolution they wanted their own copyright legislation which was written into the Constitution in 1787. Perhaps tellingly the US Copyright Clause made much more explicit the industrial importance of intellectual property. Its stated aim was:

"To promote the Progress of Science and useful Arts, by securing for limited Times to Authors and Inventors the exclusive Right to their respective Writings and Discoveries"

But America only recognised the rights of its own authors, not of foreigners.

Carey's Library of Choice Literature was launched in America in 1838 with reprints of English novels that were sold a chapter at a time. No copyright was paid to the British authors, the paper and binding were cheap and subscribers received the book through the mail at the special low prices designed for newspapers. But the US Post Office, lobbied by traditional US booksellers, decided the publication was not a newspaper at all and it would be charged at a higher rate which put it out of business

Another format of unauthorized book re-printing was then tried by an American entrepreneur called Park Benjamin. He came up with what he claimed as a weekly paper which looked and felt like a magazine called *Brother Jonathan*. And this time the Post Office allowed it. The publication carried works by the likes of Charles Dickens (who did not get paid) and quickly had more than 30,000 subscribers. Dickens like other British writers was only able to capitalize on his American popularity by doing lucrative US speaking tours. These ticketed live events were a Victorian response to illegal copying which would be repeated by the music business 150 years later when record sales slumped in the face of digital downloads and live music become a key source of income.

The success of *Brother Jonathan* led others followed suit. Publishers would wait for boats to arrive from England and literally pirate new books at the docks and have them reprinted in the cheap American format within hours. A book that might have cost a pound in London cost pennies in New York.

The publications were called "pamphlet novels" and met with much disapproval. English geologist Charles Lyle when visiting the USA commented:

"Many are of the opinion that the small print of the cheap editions in the United States will injure the eyesight of a rising generation,

especially as they are often read in railway cars, devouring whole novels, printed in newspapers in very inferior type".

British publishers responded by stealing and reprinting the works of newly popular American writers like Mark Twain. These were the low cost "yellow-back" books which were sold by the newly formed WH Smith at railway stations. In the face of all this intellectual theft in 1886 the Berne Convention, which was inspired by the French author Victor Hugo, tried to give copyright international status. But it was not until more than 100 years later in 1988 that the UK and USA passed laws to bring them fully into line with the Berne principles.[1]

Copyright or Intellectual Property ("IP") is at the heart of the economics of all media and it is no surprise that books, as the first mass medium, were the first to encounter the issues relating to ownership of ideas.

The notion that a creative artist owns the right to reproduce his or her work was extended to the visual arts and sheet music, then to recorded sound, radio, television and film. The duration of an author's or composer's copyright has been extended time and again over the past three centuries (driven by vocal lobbying by publishers and music companies). In some cases it can now be 50 years or more.

Copyright law is constantly changing to keep up with new technologies. For example the 1911 UK Copyright act gave films protection as "works of dramatic art" defined as a "series of photographs" owned by the photographer. It was not until the 1956 they were protected and defined as "films" in their own right to include script, characters and music. It was the same 1956 Act that extended copyright law to television which was, then, a relatively recent invention and initially rights were protected as there was only the BBC involved.

Copyright is always trying to achieve a balancing act between providing a creator with fair reward for their work but not prevent-

---

[1] The UK non-conformity with Berne was that pre the 1988 Act there was no statutory protection of authors' moral rights, and this was remedied in the 1988 Act. But the UK argument was that the moral rights were fully protected in common law, and the UK was a full, and original, signatory of Berne and not excluded because of this defect. The main reforming US Act was 1976, which liberalised the previously 'offensive' requirement for registration, but left in place the US manufacturing clause, which denied protection to foreign works not printed in the US. This was repealed in 1986 and the US was accepted into Berne in 1989. Clive Bradley.

ing open discussion of ideas. Limited use of copyright material – for example a quote in a newspaper or brief mention on television – can be done under what is called "fair dealing" exemptions in the UK and "fair use" in the USA.

Copyright legislators have always lagged behind technology and practice and now the advent of digital media has called this whole area of law into question. Once any medium – text, sound or video – is digitised it is exceptionally simple to make a perfect copy at almost no cost, instantly, anywhere in the world.

Chaucer was protected by the cost of writing books by hand, Shakespeare by holding onto his originals, Dickens by charging for his readings and film makers, for many years, by the cost and complexity of their medium.

The logic that led Queen Anne and her ministers to "encourage learning" still holds today. Whilst it is true that many creative people will produce simply for the love of their art, much of the very best of media content needs investment. And creative artists deserve their reward. The Web has given us huge freedom in terms of access to a huge range of global media but without some new form of copyright solution it may threaten the very creativity and invention that we all admire and enjoy.

The Directive on the Legal Protection of Databases of 11 March 1996: Does it have a Future?

LAURENCE KAYE

LAURENCE KAYE SOLICITORS, SPECIALIST IN DIGITAL MEDIA LAW

In the independently-researched Chambers UK Guide to the Legal Profession 2008, Laurence Kaye is top ranked for publishing law and highly ranked for technology law. Laurence was recently appointed as a member of the Copyright Expert Panel established by SABIP, the body which advises the UK Government on intellectual property policy. Laurence Kaye is described as a "real publishing expert" (Chambers' Guide 2009) and he recently acted on copyright, database right, privacy and e-commerce legal issues for the European Publishers Council. He now runs a niche UK legal practice specialising in digital media, technology and intellectual property law, combining in-depth industry experience with very competitive legal rates. Clients range from listed companies to individual entrepreneurs. He was one of the first lawyers in the UK to work in the field of Internet and E-business law and advises on both traditional media and 'Web 2.0/ Law2.0' issues.

Abstract: The purpose of the EU Directive on the legal protection of databases of 11 March 1996 (the Database Directive), which has now been implemented by all member states, was to create a harmonised legal regime for the protection of databases in Europe.

It did this in two ways. First, by inventing a new right – the database right (also known as the 'sui generis' right) – to protect substantial investment made by database producers in obtaining, verifying and presenting database contents. Second, it harmonised the rules governing copyright in databases. Whereas the database right protects investment, database copyright only arises where the structure of the database, including the selection and arrangement of the database's contents, meets a test of intellectual creativity on the part of the individuals who designed it.

The database right has proven to be a useful tool in protecting valuable corporate data. But it has its critics too, who accuse it of potentially 'locking up' factual information. (In fact, it does not restrict the irregular use of insubstantial amounts). Furthermore, a number of decisions of the European Court of Justice have caste doubt over the true scope of the database right.

In my view, the database right has often been misunderstood. Databases are ubiquitous in the digital world and the database right has an important role to play in protecting substantial investment in databases.

Ahead of the game?

Usually, the law plays 'catch up' in the digital world, as each technological development raises novel legal questions. With that in mind, can you think of a law in Europe which pre-dates search and social media and yet was ahead of its time, digitally speaking?

There is one – the 1996 Directive on the legal protection of databases.[1] Its origin dates back to the European Commission's far sighted 'Green Paper on Copyright in the Information Society' which was published in 1988, before the Internet had emerged from the worlds of the military and academia and before Tim Berners-Lee had developed the Web. Whilst the Green Paper's focus was on copyright, it correctly foresaw the significance of 'databases' as the storehouses of content in the information age, and the need to encourage and protect database investment. Just substitute 'website' for 'database' and you will immediately see the point.

Before the Directive was introduced, there was a mixed bag of legal protection for databases. In the UK and Netherlands, databases were protected by literary copyright as 'sweat of the brow' works such as tables or compilations. But in other European Union countries, such as Germany, they were often unprotected because they did not meet the higher threshold of authors' 'intellectual creativity' that those countries required for copyright protection.

So the solution adopted by the Database Directive was to introduce a two tier level of protection for databases. It raised the threshold for copyright in a database to a higher level of 'author's

---

[1]   Directive 96/9/EC of the European Parliament and of the Council of 11 March 1996 on the legal protection of databases.

own intellectual creation' in the 'selection and arrangement' of the database's contents. It also introduced the new 15 year, renewable database right (also known as the 'sui generis' right) to protect 'substantial investment' made by a European database producer in obtaining, verifying and presenting the database's contents.

The database right is therefore an entirely new creature of European law and has no direct counterpart outside the European Union. The Database Directive was eventually adopted by the European Council in 1996 and has been implemented by all member states. The UK implemented it by Regulation in 1998.[2]

A chequered history

However, despite this legislative foresight, the Database Directive has had a chequered legal career since it hit the statute books. In my view, the fundamental reasons are confusion about the precise scope of the legal protection given by the Directive, not helped by the often contradictory case law. Also, the European Court of Justice's decisions in the *'Fixtures Marketing'* and *'William Hill'* cases, which are discussed below, punctured a hole in the scope of protection.

The Database Directive was conceived in the 1990's and modelled on large business databases which acted as giant storehouses of data gathered from other sources, where the investment lay not in the creation of the data but in gathering, checking and presenting data. Now fast forward to today where the database right finds itself at the meeting point between technology and the law. Search engines, web scrapers, data aggregation tools, API's and a range of other Internet/Web-based technologies automate the ways in which data and other content is taken and re-used without any human intervention. One of the functions of the Database Directive – and this is no easy task – is to draw the legal boundary between activities which need permission and those which do not.

European legislators remain ambivalent about the database right, The European Commission carried out carried out its first Evaluation Report of the Database Directive in 2005.[3] It concluded that the economic impact of the database right was unproven, but opted to maintain the status quo and to leave the right unaltered.

---

[2]   The Copyright and Rights in Databases Regulations (as amended), Statutory Instrument 1997 No. 3032.
[3]   First evaluation of Directive 96/9/EC on the legal protection of databases December 2005.

Database publishers and other rights-holders shared no such doubts and believe that it remains a valuable right.

Despite these doubts, I believe that the database right has an important role to play in protecting commercially valuable data such as marketing databases, metadata and other 'added value' information on the network. Furthermore database copyright will, I believe, grow in importance as means of protection for classification systems and other 'information building blocks.

To test that assertion, in the remaining parts of this article I will examine what is (and is not) protected by the Database Directive, how the Courts have interpreted it and then make some predictions about its future.

What kinds of databases are protected under the Database Directive?

The answer is – virtually any form of collection, whether in print, fixed electronic media or online.

The Database Directive defines a 'database' very widely as "*a collection of independent works, data or other materials arranged in a systematic or methodical way and individually accessible by electronic or other means*". Case law since around 2000 has shown that websites with collections of jobs, real estate data, classified ads, directories, collections of website links and poems are all protected, as are collections in CD-ROM and paper formats too.

The Database Right

What is protected by the database right?

Database right arises if there is "*substantial investment ... in obtaining, verifying or presenting [database] contents*". 'Substantial' can be in terms of quality or quantity or both and 'investment' includes any investment whether of financial, human or technical resources. The substantial investment can be in obtaining content or verifying it or presenting it or in any combination of all three elements.

The right lasts for fifteen years from the end the year in which the database was completed. This fifteen year term can be renewed if a 'substantial change' to the database contents, judged qualitatively or quantitatively, results in the database being considered to be a substantial new investment.

It is therefore easy to see that a dynamic, regularly updated database would almost undoubtedly qualify for a fresh term of protection. However, this would not be the case with databases consisting of works which do not change e.g. an anthology containing all English love poetry of the 19th Century.

However, as we will see later on, the decisions of the European Courts of Justice in the 2004 decisions in the Fixtures Marketing cases[4] and the *William Hill* case[5] created a hole in the protection given by the database right. Essentially, they excluded from protection data which was newly created by the database owner as distinct from pre-existing data gathered from third party sources.

What rights does the database right give?

The owner of the database right can prevent the whole or substantial part of the content of the database being ;extracted' or 're-utilised' without permission. So taking 'insubstantial parts' of a database does not infringe the right.

'Extraction' is a broad concept. It means *"permanent or temporary transfer of [database] contents to another medium by any means or any form"*. Subsequent case law has shown that 'extraction' happens as soon as material is taken from a database and stored elsewhere and that infringement does not depend on the use to which someone wants to put the information.[6] Also, data is treated as being 'extracted' from a database where data it is re-keyed into another database. Physical copying, by technical means or otherwise, is not required for the right to be infringed.[7]

'Re-utilisation' means *"making contents available to the public by any means"*. So, for example, posting content onto a web site would involve 're-utilisation'.

Who owns the database right?

The database right is a producer's right. The 'maker' of the database is the first owner of the database right. The 'maker' is defined as: *"the person who takes the initiative in obtaining, verifying or presenting the*

---

[4]   Fixtures Marketing Ltd v. Organismos etc; Case C-444/02; together with two other cases involving Fixtures Marketing Ltd.

[5]   British Horseracing Board v. William Hill Organisation; Case C-203/02.

[6]   ECJ in Apis-Hristovich v. Lakorda AD.

[7]   ECJ in Directmedia Publishing GmbH v. Albert-Ludwigs-Universitat Freiburg (Case C-304/07).

contents of a database and assumes the risk of investing in that obtaining, verification or presentation shall be regarded as the maker of, and as having made, the database".

If the database has been made by an employee in the course of employment, then his employer would be regarded as the maker of the database, subject to any agreement to the contrary.

To qualify for database right, the maker must be an individual resident in the European Economic Area ('EEA') or, in the case of a company, incorporated in an EEA country when the database was made.

Exceptions to the database right

The exceptions apply to the 'lawful user' of a database. The most important exception is for fair dealing with a substantial part of its contents if it is extracted for the purpose of illustration for teaching or research and not for any commercial purpose and the source is indicated.

The hole in the database right

This was created by four decisions of the European Court of Justice (ECJ) in 2004. The first three involved Fixtures Marketing which, on behalf of the UK football leagues, licenses the fixture lists outside the UK for pools betting and other uses. The fourth was a referral by the UK Courts of the British Horseracing Board (BHB) v. William Hill case. This involved the use of information from the BHB database on the William Hill internet site for online betting.

The common theme of all these decisions by the ECJ was to deny database right protection where a database contains data created by the database producer as a 'spin off' of other activities – the compiling of football fixtures list in the case of BHB and horse racing fixtures in the other cases.

In all cases, the database owner alleged infringement of its database right in its database by the unauthorised use of its data. In all four cases the ECJ ruled that the *"investment in the obtaining, verification or presentation of the contents"* of the database refers to *"the resources used to seek out existing independent materials and collect them into the database and not to the resources used for the creation of such independent materials"*.

Put simply, the ECJ decided that if a database is a by-product of the database maker's principal activity and that the investment goes into that activity and not into the gathering together of pre-existing materials, then no sui generis protection is available! So in BHB's case, the ECJ decided that its investment went into the creation of the lists for racing, checking the identity of the person making the entry for the race and other information about the race and its entrants. All of this was part of its principal activity of organising horseracing and took place before the database was created. A similar line of reasoning appears in the three cases involving Fixtures Marketing.

Database Copyright

The purpose of the database right is to protect the investment made in the production of the data. In contrast, copyright in a database protects 'originality' on the part of the individual author(s) who created it. The test is whether: "*...by reason of the selection or arrangement of the contents of the database, the database constitutes the authors' own intellectual creation*".

This sounds very literary and a world away from XML, API's, feeds and all the other technologies used to extract data from one digital resource and display it in another. It probably is. But essentially, it's about protecting originality and creativity reflected in the design and structuring of the database (e.g. as reflected in a website) and in the selection of its contents.

Take the example of online City Guide containing factual information, illustrations (maps of a city and plans of museums), commentary and listings. If the author or authors of the guide have used skill and creativity in choosing the contents from a large range of information, and/or in the presentation and arrangement of the contents in the guide, then it is likely to meet the originality test. Essentially, it is the structure of the database which is protected by copyright. This point is expressly made in the Directive.

If the database is 'original', and therefore qualifies for protection, it will have the same term of protection as other literary works i.e. 70 years from the date of death of the author or, in the case of several authors, the last surviving author. Generally speaking, it is also subject to the same exceptions as other literary works.

The Future for the Database Directive

The Database Directive undoubtedly has its critics and the continuing uncertainty about its scope, especially in the light of the William Hill and Fixtures Marketing cases, does not help. It would certainly benefit database producers and users if these could be clarified.

Furthermore, the database right is at the moment only a creature of European law. That is a challenge in a globally networked world.

But notwithstanding those reservations, I firmly believe that this legal 'problem child' will mature. The reasons that led to the introduction of the database right remain as valid today as they were when the right was first conceived in the late 1980's. There is huge value invested in databases as networked-based resources of all types of content, whether as collections of valuable business data, copyright materials or hybrids.

The database right was designed to protect substantial investment and does not prevent the irregular taking of insubstantial parts of a database. It does not 'lock up' data as some critics maintain and, in my view, strikes an appropriate balance. For these reasons, the Database Directive deserves to come of age in the 21st century.

Enlightenment Now

DOMINIC McGONIGAL

DIRECTOR OF PUBLIC AFFAIRS, PPL

Abstract: 300 years ago, copyright was a radical concept. It generated disputes in the early days and has periodically inspired controversy ever since, culminating in the abolitionists of the dotcom boom. Ten years ago, the futurists were predicting the demise of copyright. But is copyright dead, or is this the coming of age for this concept, which still feels new after three centuries?

Certainly, the Digital Age has challenged the notion of ownership, when the entire music catalogue is now available, online, free and illegal. When consumers can circumvent normal rules and get everything free, what is the future for copyright? How can artists reap their just reward from their work?

The answer lies in the hidden business activities in the creative industries in the past few decades. Out of the limelight of the digital revolution, a range of licensing models have been developed to deal with the conflicting demands of ever increasing volumes coupled with simplicity and flexibility. The paradoxes are evident. Creative work is consumed more than ever, yet creators' income is falling. Can licensing bridge this gap? Does copyright have a role in the Digital Age? Are we now living in the true Age of Enlightenment?

Enlightenment Now

Ten years ago, at the height of the dotcom boom, the futurists were predicting the demise of copyright. Those futurists can now skip to the final paragraph to see if they were right. Others might take a journey through the ages and wonder if this is anything new.

300 years ago, copyright was a radical concept, breaking through in the dawn of the Enlightenment. Our forefathers broke the old monopoly system and gave authors control of what they wrote. Queen Anne granted "the Author of any Book or Books ... the sole Right and Liberty of Printing such Book and Books." For the first time, authors had the essential bargaining chip, ownership of their work, when negotiating with the booksellers. They could trade own-

ership of their work in return for royalties, advances or other benefits.

It is interesting to speculate as to what predictions were made back in 1710 as this new concept was introduced into statute. Certainly there were disputes between booksellers as to nature of copyright granted by the new statute. In time, history confirmed it as a property right which increased the trade in books, based on their intrinsic value rather than an artificial monopoly on production and distribution.

As the Enlightenment gave way to the Industrial Revolution, markets grew and production mechanised to meet growing demand. Copyright remained the mainstay of authors' agreements, but it was contractual provisions through the distribution chain which controlled the economics of the business. Copyright became the subject of debate again in the 19th century with Charles Dickens deploring the rampant piracy in the original Wild West of America, where there were no copyright laws and Thomas McCauley describing it as 'the least objectionable way of remunerating' authors in a debate in the House of Commons. Copyright was still not universally accepted. It was significant then that all the major trading nations met in Berne in 1886 to sign the first international copyright treaty. In the 20th century, international treaties were developed to cover all forms of creative work and their exploitation.

However, throughout these three centuries, from 1710 to 1999, copyright underpinned a renaissance of creative output and ever wider access to literary and musical work, resulting in creative industries which form an essential element in a modern economy. Yet, copyright remained largely hidden from public view, buried in artists' contracts, distributor agreements and High Court judgements. Copyright infringers were generally rival businesses or illegal operators out to defraud the artists' business partners.

Then, along came the Digital Age. In 1999, Napster launched and the entire catalogue of the music industry was available, online, free and illegally. Suddenly it became possible for anyone to take, first, a music track, then a TV programme, then a film, a computer game and even a whole catalogue. Consumers met copyright and it was not a marriage made in heaven. Rather than 'yes, we can', the first experience was 'no, you can't'. By the time the legal services were readily available some five years later, people had already become used to circumventing the normal rules and getting everything free.

All the accepted behaviour of the High Street had been usurped in a no-questions-asked culture online.

The digital utopians leapt on this and declared that copyright was dead. They wanted to mix and match with impunity. They heralded a new age when users would generate their own content. The creator is dead, long live the user.

But is copyright dead? Or are the digital utopians simply wearing the Emperor's new clothes?

In the digital environment, all we have to trade are intangibles. Some of that is raw fact and information. The more interesting material is the smart arrangement of that information and the creations of the heart and the mind.

How do you reward an artist, when a work can be accessed almost anywhere by anyone? How do you retain a link between an artist and their work when it can be cached on a billion computers? Throughout the Enlightenment and the Industrial Age, distribution channels could be controlled and there was a contractual chain from consumer back to artist via a handful of intermediaries. In the Digital Age, a track can be available to billions of consumers from the moment it is released and once it is out there, the artist and their business partners often have no relationship with the end user. Control of a distribution channel no longer works.

And yet, that track, that book, that film, that game still has a value. Arguably its value has increased as more people access it, listen to it, read it, watch it or play with it. It has been freed from its physical shackles and can be enjoyed for what it is. A creative work. A piece of copyright.

That's where the 18th century concept of ownership comes into its own. If you know that the recording you see on your file menu belongs to those who created it, there is an automatic obligation to the artists and producers. You can't take someone else's work, just because it is convenient to you. These principles are well established in the physical world, but we have yet to accommodate them in the virtual environment. It is not the concept of copyright that is dead in the digital age. It is the application of that fundamental principle – that you own what you create – which is yet to be fully realised online.

The key to application of copyright in the Digital Age is licensing. It is licensing which converts the concept of value in a creative work into a reality. Licensing establishes a two-way relationship between user and rightholder, no longer reliant on industrial distribution chains, but rather on the intrinsic value of the work to both consumer and artist.

It is easy for history to assign a date to a revolution – 1789 in Paris, 1914 in Sarajevo, 1933 in Berlin, 1999 on the Internet – but change is never as tidy as that. Just as there is a lag as the world catches up, there are pre-cursors that set the agenda for future generations. Thus, throughout the second half of the 20th century, new licensing models were developing, designed initially for a highly mechanised world where production costs tended towards zero, but equally applicable to a network world where large-scale distribution becomes generally available.

The transformation of music publishing is a case in point. In the 1950s, the sheet music chart was what counted and the business of the music publisher was to reproduce, distribute and sell large quantities of their composers' work in printed form. By the 1960s, the record chart had taken over and sheet music sales plummeted. Within a space of ten years, their business had moved from control of a distribution channel to licensing the music itself. What mattered then was the value of the song, to the user and to the composer.

Licensing now takes many forms and is arguably most developed within the music industry, although new structures have emerged recently in book publishing and photographic libraries. At one end there is an individual licence for a single work for specific uses. An iconic recording in an advert gives enormous value to the brand and consequently attracts a significant payment in a sync licence. At the other end of the scale are the collective licences where a whole catalogue is bundled in a single licence for multiple use. Radio is the classic example where each trackplay generates a small payment, but those payments are aggregated in an annual licence and paid through a collective licensing body. Effectively, the collective licensing society acts as a clearing house between the millions of listeners hearing hundreds of thousands of tracks and the tens of thousands of performers and record companies who have created and invested in those tracks.

More recently, variants of these two models have been developed to deal with the increasing demands of simplicity and speed. The aim of each is to assess the value of a particular use and return that to the creator, usually using a consumption metric generating royalty payments. It is a dynamic pricing model that is flexible in relation to changing levels of use. Increasingly, the trend has been to reduce the transaction costs to a minimum so that the true value of the work is realised, rather than the incidental physical and administrative costs.

One particularly imaginative variant was developed around twenty years ago in the UK. It addressed the most difficult area, where the potential conflict between public demands for unimpeded use and creators' concern for the value and integrity of their material was most acute. This was the use of TV programmes in the classroom. No one doubted that children should have access to this valuable resource. The challenge was finding a solution which allowed teachers to incorporate any programme in the curriculum whilst ensuring the rightholders received their fair dues. All the while, the transaction drag had to be kept to a minimum. The result was an 'exception subject to licence' introduced into the 1988 Copyright Act. A year later, the Educational Recording Agency was founded, offering a single annual licence to schools, returning the revenue to all the contributors – the broadcasters, the authors, the actors, the artists and the producers. That is a model that is being considered in other similar statutory situations.

We enter the Digital Age then with an apparent paradox. Creative work is consumed more than ever, yet creators' income is falling. Licensing models exist to deal with the scale and breadth of the networked world, yet online piracy remains the norm. Something is missing. There is a break in the chain. And it is the gaps we have allowed in copyright.

Our forefathers in the Age of the Enlightenment gave authors ownership of their books and largely left them to work things out with the booksellers and others. Our best intentions in accommodating other worthy interests has compromised that ownership and left havens where respect for the artist can be overlooked.

So, were the futurists right? Is copyright dead? No. The Digital Age is the apotheosis of the Age of Enlightenment. Creative work is free of physical shackles. It is copyright which allows its true commercial value to shine through. The challenge now for legislators and others is to allow ownership to take its course so creators can reap the just rewards of their labour for another three centuries. Once we to do that, we will have the truly enlightened age envisaged by our forebears.

Copyright in the Digital Environment: a Broadcaster's Perspective

NAJMA RAJAH

SENIOR ECONOMIC ADVISER, POLICY AND STRATEGY, BBC

Najma has been working for the BBC since May 2007 as a Senior Economic Adviser in Policy and Strategy. During that time she has worked closely with colleagues responsible for negotiating with the talent unions, music collecting societies, photographic agencies, museums and galleries and organisations representing writers. Prior to working at the BBC, Najma worked as an economic consultant within the private sector and in the civil service.

Abstract: This article looks at some of the key challenges to the current copyright framework posed by the transition to digital technologies. It considers the impact that technological change has had on the ways in which broadcasters deliver content and the ways in which the audience access content and how digital technologies have redefined what creative content is. It reflects on the challenges that these changes pose for copyright law and contracting rights – particularly in terms of their impact on piracy within the television industry. The article concludes with a discussion of some potential solutions to these problems based on modifications to the existing copyright framework. For example, measures to permit the regulated use of orphan works which at present cannot be used without infringing copyright, provisions to allow certain collecting societies to set up extended collective licensing schemes, and reforms to the current Satellite and Cable Directive.

Copyright in the Digital Environment: a Broadcaster's View

It is very timely that that the Stationers' Company has put together a report to commemorate the 300th anniversary of the Statute of Anne. Until recently debate about copyright policy had mainly been viewed as being the preserve of lawyers. However, the subject has recently emerged from the shadows to sit at the forefront of public policy, culminating in the recent discussions around the Digital Economy Bill. One of the reasons for this is the importance that copyright plays in fostering creativity, helping to incentivise the creation of new works by ensuring that authors are rewarded for their efforts.

Creativity is also central to the BBC mission to inform, educate and entertain. In the absence of a robust and flexible copyright regime, the BBC would be less able to create, use and exploit the rights required to broadcast over 23,000 network hours of television and 78,000 network hours of radio per year. Nor would it be in a position to make available such a wide range of content on its website, bbc.co.uk, which last year on average reached 26.6 million unique users each week.

Copyright and rights payments are highly significant to the BBC. The BBC is a major contributor to the UK creative industries, spending approximately £2.4 billion per annum on original content and £1billion of that is spent on rights. The programmes that the BBC commission cover a broad range of talent, contributors and underlying rights that shape and define the BBC's output. Some individual programming (e.g. a major drama or documentary) can involve several hundred contributors. In 2007/08 the BBC issued 305,000 contracts to contributors for in-house programming alone and each week some 250,000 items of music are reported to the Music Collecting Societies.

The present UK copyright framework has largely served broadcasters and those involved in the content creation chain well, rewarding and recognising creative endeavour, whilst at the same time encouraging creativity and innovation. However, the world has moved on. The introduction of digital technology has heralded a fundamental change in the way consumers watch content; for instance Video on Demand services, such as the BBC iPlayer, have transformed audiences' ability to access content when they want. At the same time, technological change has made it easier and quicker for consumers to create and copy content in ways that were not previously possible, giving rise to phenomena such as peer-to-peer file sharing and online streaming of channels.

Government, both at a UK and European level, has acknowledged that the current regime will need to evolve. In November 2009 the UK Intellectual Property Office (IPO) published ©*the way ahead: a strategy for copyright in the digital age* and in October 2009 the European Union (EU) published a reflection paper entitled *Creative Content in a Single European Market: Challenges for the Future.*

Key challenges in a digital age

There are some common themes across both documents. Both recognise the importance of copyright and the value of the creative industries more generally. A key objective of the IPO strategy is to ensure that the copyright system supports creativity and promotes investment and jobs. Similarly the EU reflection paper states that copyright is one of the cornerstones of Europe's cultural heritage and of a culturally diverse and economically vibrant creative content sector.

Likewise both papers agree that technological changes have altered the way that broadcasters deliver and the way that consumers access content. Traditionally, television was broadcast using analogue signals, digital signals (terrestrial, cable and satellite) were introduced in the late 1990s, and now we are currently enjoying the 'third age' of distribution via mobile platforms and the internet.

But changes in distribution platforms have had implications for copyright. For example, in the old analogue world, a programme would be reused if it were repeated. In the new digital world, reusing content may require it to be available over the internet. And there are other instances of where transition from a analogue to a digital world has required a reinterpretation of the terms used in the context of copyright.

As well as giving multiple means of access, digital technologies have redefined what creative content actually is. In the past, programme-making involved studios and expensive cameras. Now it is possible to create videos at home and share copyright works across the world in seconds with friends and family. There are now almost limitless opportunities for both the use as well as distribution of creative content.

These changes have created challenges for copyright law and contracting rights. The problem of piracy, in the past more associated with the film and the music industries, is growing increasingly more important in the television industry. The UK has been described as a world leader in TV piracy with 25% of all online piracy taking place here – partly because English is a global language.[1] Television Against Piracy research put the total loss from piracy for the TV industry as £82 million in 2007.

---

[1] See Online piracy – downloading the facts, Mediatique (2009), http://www.mediatique.co.uk/reports/piracy.pdf.

Against this backdrop, it is perhaps not surprising that policy-makers have asked content creating industries to consider how the copyright framework could evolve to reflect these challenges.

Achieving a copyright framework for the digital age

The BBC believes that some of the proposals currently on policy-makers' agenda represent useful steps in the right direction.

In particular, measures to allow for the introduction of extended licensing schemes will simplify rights clearance, particularly where broadcasters are seeking to make archive material available to the public on new platforms and services in the digital environment. These schemes will enable approved licensing bodies or 'collecting societies' to license works, not only where authorised by members of the collecting society but also where the copyright owners are not members (unless they have specifically vetoed the use of their works). This is the rationale behind statutory schemes which have been operating successfully in Denmark and other Nordic countries since the 1960's and have facilitated the emergence of successful new catch-up, on-demand and archive services in Scandinavia.

In addition, proposed measures to permit the regulated use of orphan works – that is, those works for whom the rights-holder cannot be found which, at present, cannot be used without infringing copyright – will allow a licensing body 'or other person' in future to license use of orphan works. If adopted, these changes will remove a significant barrier to public access to creative works. The BBC estimates that it has around 500,000 documents, 4 million photographs and approximately 1 million hours of broadcast footage in its archive. The BBC goes through a detailed process of trying to establish who owns the rights to all these items (including all the components that contribute to individual programmes), but inevitably that is not always possible to trace all authors. As a result, many cultural assets remain under lock and key because of the legal difficulties associated with using these works.

Taken together, these two proposals will greatly simplify rights clearance whilst at the same time ensuring that rights-holders get a fair return for their creative endeavours. They will provide important benefits for broadcasters who, at the moment, need to clear individually for the archive most of the underlying rights included in their archive programmes for new services. In practice this involves the near impossible task of obtaining permission to use rights on a retrospective basis for scripts, performances, directors' rights, music, film clips, sound recordings, photographs, fine art and other copyright works, all of which may have different owners for different types of use.

The European Union's Reflection Paper also includes some helpful proposals – such as proposals to extend the Satellite and Cable Directive to other platforms. The 1993 Satellite and Cable (SATCAB) Directive has performed well, complementing the Television Without Frontiers Directive in delivering cross-border provision of television services insofar as this could be achieved under the technological and market conditions of the past 15 years. But its restricted focus on cable and satellite makes the SATCAB Directive outdated in the internet age. If the Directive and its underlying principles are to be future-proofed and deliver benefits to a post-2010 Europe, it must be modernised on the basis of technology- and platform-neutrality, and multi-territoriality. This will require two steps.

First, the regime established for cable retransmission could be extended to enable the simultaneous, unaltered and unabridged retransmission of broadcasts by third parties via any media platform. Therefore the non-cable platform operator, like the cable operator now, would need to clear the retransmission rights only with the originating broadcaster on the one hand and the collecting societies for the remaining rights on the other. This would significantly ease rights clearance for platforms such as mobile, satellite and IPTV, thereby creating a level playing field.

Second, the 'country of origin of the transmission' rule used for satellite could be extended to all audiovisual media communications on all platforms. For some time contractual arrangements would likely often continue to restrict content to individual member states on the basis of business needs and audience demand. But this modernisation of EU law would nonetheless encourage innovation in retransmission services and multi-territorial or EU-wide provision of content. As already highlighted, innovation is progressing very rapidly. Adapting the Cable and Satellite Directive would undoubtedly remove a disincentive to treating audiovisual distribution via the internet differently from traditional broadcasting, and encourage a multiplatform approach to distribution both globally and, by reflection, nationally.

Although the reforms listed above are based on changes to the existing copyright legislation, their impact on opening up access to licence fee funded content will be significant whilst at the same time ensuring that creators are rewarded. The BBC has an ambition to make more of its archive universally available over the internet over the next ten years, creating an engine for new public value – connecting audiences with the best of everything that the BBC has ever made. These reforms will be critical in enabling the BBC to achieve this ambition.

Copyright in Practice: The Publisher Perspective

KEVIN TAYLOR

DIRECTOR OF STRATEGY AND INTELLECTUAL PROPERTY,
CAMBRIDGE UNIVERSITY PRESS

Kevin Taylor is Director of Strategy and Intellectual Property at Cambridge University Press, where he has global responsibility for all IP matters including contracts, rights administration, permissions, copyright policy and copyright protection. Previously, as publishing director in the humanities & social sciences group, he ran a team responsible for seven academic subject areas.

Kevin graduated from the University of Cambridge with a first class honours degree in English in 1984 and joined the Press a few days later. His other roles in the company have included senior commissioning editor (literature), editorial manager of reference publishing, and manager of the electronic publishing unit. He is meetings secretary to the University Press Syndicate.

In the UK publishing industry Kevin has served as a board director of the Copyright Licensing Agency, the Publishers Licensing Society, and the Academic & Professional Division of the Publishers Association. He has also written a best-selling historical guidebook, Central Cambridge: A Guide to the University and Colleges *(second edition 2008); edited a University exhibition catalogue,* Foundations for the Future *(1995); and is the author of numerous articles and talks about publishing.*

Abstract: Copyright is entering a transitional phase, and there is much debate about its future role in the digital world. Practising publisher Kevin Taylor discusses the complex nature of copyright, arguing that changes must occur, but gradually. 'Content' (the author's creative expression) is only one element of copyright, and numerous other kinds of value are in play in the complex chain of protection and exploitation that characterises the distribution of a copyrighted work. Increased threats from e-piracy and from technological innovators such as Google pose a challenge to publishers, who must think creatively about their own role in the chain and find ways of applying their traditional values in an altered environment.

Copyright in Practice: The Publisher Perspective

Copyright is facing more concerted challenges than in any of its previous three hundred years on the statute books; but copyright has never been simple, and calls for its modification must take account of the complexity of the ideas that have characterised its evolution over three centuries.

It has been said that copyright is actually two rights: the creative right of the author; and the further assertions and exploitations of that right by publishers and others in an extended value-chain. A tension lies in the very etymology of the word. The "copyright" belonging to the creator of a work is not in fact the "right to copy" as may be expected from the lexical formation, but rather the "right to grant the right to copy". The actual "right to copy" is that which is acquired from the creator by a licensee. The creator – usually an author – grants to the licensee – usually a publisher – a contractual "right to copy" in consideration of certain terms and conditions. The publisher then sells on to its own customers a value-enhanced version of the copyrighted material in consideration of payment by the customer of the price of the book. The chain might extend further. If the customer is a library, it will pass lending rights on to its members; if the customer is a wholesaler or other intermediary it will sell the book on to a retail outlet; if the customer is a bookshop it will sell the book to an individual reader.

In each step of this chain of value-exchange, the first party has a different interest in the copyright to the second. As the owner of the work, the author is concerned to maximise the value of the creation – be that a monetary measure or a distributional one or a combination of the two. The publisher acquiring the work will want to pay for it as little as is compatible with maintaining good relations with the author. But then in the next step of the chain the roles change as the publisher becomes concerned to protect and exploit the copyright in the same ways that the author has in the previous step. At each step, value is added to the commodity.

A tension between protection and exploitation has always lain at the heart of copyright. Most authors want to ensure that their creation is properly valued while at the same time ensuring their work's best possible distribution. Publishing is about the practical management of that tension, and copyright has provided the regulatory framework in which it plays out. How to distribute a book as effectively as possible while maximising the return? Over the years, publishers have evolved sophisticated models for getting this right.

The tension is more pronounced than ever in a world where technology is increasingly 'problematising' traditional chains of value. It is easy for an author to make his own work available on the internet; likewise for a pirate to copy a work electronically and mass-distribute it in e-form. I deal daily with authors who want both to post their work on their own free-to-access website and to earn the highest possible royalties from sales of the same work; authors who argue for the widest possible dissemination of their book while deploring its theft by pirates who distribute it widely but in devalued forms. It is understandable that authors should find themselves on the horns of a dilemma when technology both promotes and threatens their interests to such an unprecedented degree.

Technology is re-shaping the sphere in which traditional regulatory controls have operated; but calls for the radical modification or even abolition of those controls deny the complexity of the origin and history of copyright, the balance of tensions which have made it a successful form of regulation for so long, and the fact that those tensions continue to exist – arguably in heightened form – in a world dominated by technology. We recall that aspect of copyright which has its origins in the French Enlightenment and in the common-law rights pre-dating Queen Anne, arising from the creative need of the individual to communicate his or her ideas and to be identified as their owner. Challenges to copyright strike at the heart not only of publishers' business models but at the very notion of authorship, and there are long-entrenched senses of literary proprietorship at stake as well as publishers' balance sheets.

Open Access and the Creative Commons movement are often cited as a threat to traditional publishing, yet it is notable that such models do not fundamentally undermine copyright. Publishers can and do work constructively with concepts such as self-archiving, and are evolving new cost models that respect the desire of academics to have ready access to their own content. An author's right to be credited and to retain control over the effects of his creative expression are built into these models.

The creative industries account for a huge proportion of the GDP of developed countries, and a rapidly increasing slice of the economies of the developing world. The investment in traditional configurations of author and publisher is too great, the vested interests too large, for change to occur overnight. One thing we have learned is that there are no tipping-points. The inertia in the system is too considerable to allow for radical change. Change must occur, as the music industry has discovered; but that industry did not collapse. The models are evolving and the regulatory environment subtly shifting; but people still make music and profit from doing so.

The same will be true of books. Perhaps the biggest recent threat to traditional copyright has come from Google's mass-digitisation project; but it is telling that this has not precipitated any immediate momentous change. It has resulted instead in a highly complex Settlement proposal which shows evidence of all the tensions between protection and exploitation that have characterised copyright over the years, and which as I write is generating more confusion than consensus with no sign of imminent resolution.

It is likely that the Google Settlement will come to be regarded as one of those thresholds in the evolution of copyright on a par with long-running historic legal cases like *Donaldson v. Beckett* (1770s) – in which key distinctions were established between common-law and statutory aspects of copyright – and *Jeffreys v. Boosey* (1850s) – in which cross-border copyright was first clarified. In whatever form the Settlement is agreed, and even if it is not, it will have served as a catalyst to re-order the legislative landscape around copyright. We have known for years that the digital environment would entail a review of exceptions such as 'fair use', but it takes a forcible challenge to generate new thinking. Google's claim that its wholesale copying and snippet-display of in-copyright materials constitutes fair use will remain unresolved, even if the Settlement is approved, and that challenge will undoubtedly recur, if not from Google then from another giant technological re-shaper of cultural norms. One of the objections to the Settlement is that as a Class Action it should be addressing historical wrongs rather than attempting (as it does through the proposed Book Rights Registry) to prescribe future models – but such prescription does not emerge in a vacuum, and if the challenge has arisen on this scale then something must be in need of change.

Copyright will survive. How then must it evolve and adapt? One way will be through greater standardisation. The expansion of digital communication and the globalisation of trade both work against a copyright law determined by national jurisdiction, and cross-border issues now loom large. Harmonisation of the term to 70 years post-mortem auctoris in the EU and US was a step towards international consistency, but there remain issues for publishers attempting to protect their copyright in places like India where cultural and economic attitudes towards what might constitute 'fair use' are bound to be very different. The legal issues raised by the Google Settlement call out for global solutions and yet are awkwardly limited to the US. Complicated and sometimes unresolvable jurisdictional challenges are posed by the prevalence of internet infringement. And the viability of the system of transnational bilateral agreements which has thus far sustained the activity of collective licensing societies is increasingly called into question. All of this must tend in the future toward greater convergence if rights are to be manageable in the digital world.

The 'exceptions' allowed under copyright law (including fair use) are rightly receiving close attention, and this is another area where change will occur. More robust definitions suited to an age of global electronic distribution are required, and legislators are likely to conduct a fundamental re-examination of the intent behind the Berne Convention's 'three-step test'.

'Orphan works' must be freed up. The proposals in the Google Settlement for dealing with what are there called 'Unclaimed Works' will again serve to force the issue, and has already catalysed an EU response in the form of ARROW (Accessible Registries of Rights Information and Orphan Works). Collective licensing is evolving rapidly, with some fillips from legislation such as the UK's Digital Economy Bill. Meanwhile piracy is rampant and unstoppable – but then it always was.

The dispute between Google and rights-holders is not the first clash of powerful vested interests over intellectual property (and in the current context it might be apt to recall the long-running battles between the Stationers' Company and the University Presses, who for significant periods of the seventeenth and eighteenth centuries vied to assert their different interpretations of copyright). Nor will it be the last. Yet critics of traditional publisher-driven models must note that raw content (the author's creative expression) is only one part of the picture, and that numerous other kinds of value are in play in this complex chain of protection and exploitation.

It is undeniable that the role of the publisher is mutating from 'content distributor' to 'service provider'. As technology makes the traditional 'distribution of content' function easier, publishers are freed to focus more attention on other aspects of the value they add, and the best will regard this as an opportunity rather than a threat. In the digital age the qualities of content selection, validation, authority, editorial input, design, sales and marketing, bibliographic metadata, format standards, and brand/imprint are no less important – indeed are arguably more important – than in the print world. The reconfiguration of these qualities within a framework of technological innovation is what now drives the missions of many publishers.

The music industry eventually discovered that the best way to preserve legitimate trade in copyrighted materials was not by reactively tackling infringement but by providing viable legal alternatives for customers wanting to download music electronically. The same principle applies to books, which is why publishers are so actively developing and experimenting with electronic channels-to-market. There will always be copyright infringement, but the majority of consumers will prefer legitimate services if these are attractively packaged, readily available and reasonably priced. Our challenge is to ensure that there will be a legitimate commercial e-space for the effective dissemination of copyright-protected materials that serves the best interests of authors while fulfilling the publisher's mission to make work available through a value-adding chain of publication – just as we have always done in the print world.

As visionary US author and internet guru Clay Shirky remarked in an article for *Publishers Weekly*:

> *"As all media goes digital, the only real calamity that could befall publishers would be for them to abandon those [traditional] values."*

Three hundred years after the Act of Queen Anne, copyright faces some fundamental changes. It will however continue to provide a form of regulation that will underpin the activities of both authors and publishers in the digital world.

Why Copyright is still Important after 300 Years

IAIN STEVENSON

CENTRE FOR PUBLISHING, UNIVERSITY COLLEGE LONDON

Iain Stevenson is Professor of Publishing and Director of Teaching at the University College London (UCL's) Centre for Publishing and is Leader of the award-winning UCL MA in Publishing, established in 2006. Since gaining a PhD at UCL in 1981 he has had extensive publishing industry experience with Longman, Macmillan, Pinter, Leicester University Press, Wiley, and The Stationery Office. He has been consultant to The British Library and London Transport Users' Committee, International IDEA, and the Australian Sustainable Tourism Publishing Company. He created the award winning MA in Publishing Studies at City University London and was Senior Tutor for Research and Professor of Publishing Studies in the Department of Journalism and Publishing there between 1999 and 2006. He was active on the governing and advisory boards of the Publishers Association and the Royal Geographical Society. He founded the environmental publisher Belhaven Press in 1986. A Fellow of the Royal Geographical Society, Iain Stevenson has published much on the history of cartographic publishing and the history of scientific and educational publishing . His current research is centred upon the history of British publishing especially scientific, technical and medical publishing and publishing in Scotland concentrating on cartography. He also researches the applications of new technology in publishing, especially e-books and alternatives to the printed monograph in academic and scholarly communication. He is consultant to the forthcoming BBC Radio 4 series 'The People's Post' to be broadcast in 2011. His new book, Book Makers: British Publishing in the Twentieth Century, *was published by British Library Publishing in Spring 2010.*

Abstract: This article argues that copyright is even more important today than it was 300 years ago. The principles introduced by the statute of Anne of property rights in creative works being vested in the creator and those rights having an exclusive duration to protect their exploitation remain fundamental in the digital age. As creativity is challenged by those who would replace an orderly and fair intellectual property regime with a free for all, it is essential for copyright to be defended and strengthened. Not everything about the current legislative framework is however essential and the article proposes some amendments and changes to duration and the treatment of orphan works.

Why Copyright is still important after 300 years

When this year we celebrate the world's first copyright law formally known as "Anne" and more euphonically as the 'Statute of Anne' there is perhaps slight frisson of unease that troubles the minds of those of us who make our livings by the creation of literary property and its commercial exploitation . In its day, the Statute was a true emancipatory Act, allowing a ragged, haggard and much put-upon class of humanity to emerge from the shadows and claim at least part of their due entitlement. Hitherto, writers as a group were exploited shamefully by printers, publishers, readers and booksellers. They had no property rights in what they created and even if their works were runaway successes they did not share in its continued revenue. Anyone other than the creator was enriched by the sales of their work. Only lately had John Milton received the miserly sum of £5 for the entire interest in his great epic *Paradise Lost*. Poets, playwrights and pamphleteers starved in garrets, romantically in the imagination but in the direst poverty and degradation in reality and if a young man or woman dreamed of a literary career they had better have had private means. Not for nothing were writers known popularly as 'hacks': like mistreated hired horses they subsisted on scraps, were brutally treated and abused and once they had outlived their usefulness they were abandoned and neglected.

The Statute of Anne introduced two important new ideas. First that the creators of literary works should have an automatic right of property in those works that could not be arbitrarily removed, although like other real property it could be sold, inherited or rented. Secondly that property right had a duration—the term of copyright—over which the copyright owner had an exclusive right to the enjoyment of a share of the proceeds of the created property and if it was misappropriated, there was a right of redress. Over the next three hundred years, the rights were extended to music, artwork, drama, cinema, broadcasting, computer programmes and electronic games, all the fruits of human intellectual endeavour, and the duration was extended to reach the current seventy years after the year in which the creator dies Other rights, the so-called moral rights, to require that the author be recognised as such on the piece created (*paternity*) and the right not to have the work altered and incorporated without permission (*integrity*) appeared although the other more exotic moral rights found in some European jurisdictions like *droit de suite* (the right for the original artist to be compensated if a work is sold on nor sadly the right to protect parody)have not found favour in the legislation of the land that created copyright.

Virtuously sub-titled 'An Act for the Encouragement of Learning', Anne is actually much more important than that. Had it not been enacted, would it really have been possible to imagine the invention of the novel a few decades later, and the inevitable emergence of the legions of great professional writers who could live by their pen like Fielding, Austen, Scott, Dickens and Stevenson down to contemporaries like Mantel, Rowling and Pullman? Would the western literary canon ever have existed if authors had no right to own their work, and would publishers have been created to make it happen? Would Dr Johnson have embarked on his great dictionary, or Charles Darwin explained the origin of species without being able to reserve their rights? Would maps have been made, scientific discoveries pursued, inventions created, diseases eradicated, music made, plays performed, even democracy proclaimed had their been no polity of intellectual property, copyright and its near cousins patents and trade marking? These are big claims I know but it is truly hard to imagine the modern world in anything like its present form without the enactment and subsequent development of the regime founded on Anne.

Yet why do I suggest that as we celebrate Anne's tercentenary we do so with a sense of unease? Because everywhere copyright is under attack, and there are pervasive, if not persuasive, calls for its modification, curtailment and even abandonment. We live, so runs the argument, in a virtual world without boundaries where the World Wide Web as the graphic and interactive dimension of the internet of interlinked computers is everywhere and nowhere and thus cannot be controlled, legislated for or punished. We stand on the brink of an even more elusive and abusive world known as Web 3.0 where all the world's content and ideas will reside in amorphous clouds accessible only through the technology owned and maintained by private and unaccountable behemoths like Google and Microsoft. Surely, copyright has had its day and should now on its three hundredth birthday graciously bow out and follow the example of abacuses, whalebone stays and quill pens, picaresque and irrelevant anachronisms, and quit the stage, leaving the world to modern ways of doing things?

Dangerous and pernicious nonsense

I argue most strongly that this is dangerous and pernicious nonsense. Copyright has never been more important and more vital at the beginning of the third millennium than at any other time in its long history. The protection of the ownership and use of content created by the human intellect is today more in need of strengthening and extending than at any point in its history and like many other worthy and useful institutions it is under attack often by those who should be its guardians. Rather than feeling uneasy and apologetic, the friends of copyright should be proud, militant and combative.

Why is the defence of copyright so important? A recent estimate claimed that anything between eight and ten per cent of Britain's Gross Domestic Product arose from the creative industries which of course depend on a strong intellectual property regime to protect their economic security. In an increasingly competitive world, Britain leads the way in publishing, computer gaming, theatre and pharmaceuticals. From less than two per cent of the world's population this country produces fifteen per cent of the world's books and our creation of literature is unquestionably the best in the world. Only if writers, designers and inventors are protected and fairly recompensed can we expect to continue to punch above our weight and hope to recover national prosperity.

It is also a matter of morality and fairness. The new attack dogs who seek to undermine or abolish copyright be they respectable and legal like Google or dishonest or predatory like Pirate Bay and the legion of illegal file sharers share one common characteristic. Fundamentally they are parasites. They create nothing new, they organise (sometimes brilliantly like Google), they distribute, they take, but they do not make, they do not create, they do not make something new. If the way of the future is to be constant recycling, endless Google searching, unrestricted plagiarism and piracy, then human progress comes to a juddering halt. Humanity loses its creative spark and the only ideas are old ones constantly warmed over.

The arguments against copyright are well rehearsed. Even if it is a good thing, it cannot be policed in a borderless electronic world say the critics. In the Internet age, everyone is happy to be an author and to have their work shared for free. Wikis are the new publishers, free for all and unshackled. Blogs and social networking are done for enjoyment not recompense. All you need to address the world and become the next Herman Melville (or indeed Adolf Hitler) is a cheap laptop and an IP address. Google is being selfless and philanthropic by digitising all the world's books (and of course controlling access to them-free now but for how long?). Copyleft and Creative Commons are all the protections the world's authors, composers, performers, academics, pop groups, artists, designers, scientists, poets and knowledge workers need. Of course and they had better believe in the tooth fairy, Father Christmas and Mother Goose as well, just to be sure.

Copyright pirates: thieves, cheats and criminals

All arrant nonsense of course. Copyright needs to be made stronger and more easily regulated to ensure that in a digital world, quality content is disseminated fairly and in a timely manner, assuring to its creators just rewards. Other systems have large loopholes and are ultimately unenforceable. Copyright pirates will always seek to loot content for their own benefit but should be seen for what they are: thieves, cheats and criminals who steal the creative work of others solely for their own benefit without scruple. In a digital world, copyright is in fact enforceable as for example the widespread success of 'notice and takedown' control of infringing websites has shown. Even seemingly all-powerful Copyright refuseniks like Google can be shown the error of their ways and if not completely house-trained they do at least begin to show some continence. The recent settlement between Google and the Association of American Publishers may be impenetrable and inconclusive but it has at least equipped the publishers with a pooper scooper. It is not without significance that the very last law passed by the outgoing Brown administration in April 2010 was the much contested Digital Economy Act which introduced important copyright safeguards for owners of creative works and may in its way ultimately become a Statute of Anne for the twenty-first century.

This is of course not to argue that all is perfect in the present administration of copyright. The framers of Anne, or indeed the Acts of 1912, 1956 and 1988 which underpin the current regime would be amazed by the problems and issues that copyright holders now face, and the definitions and procedures they enacted do now look outmoded. The Digital Economy Act is only a beginning and an imaginative new approach is needed to create a workable and flexible copyright system that continues to benefit those who work by brain. Key problems are what to do about orphan works, where the author is dead, the work is out of print and there are no traceable heirs. The creative industries should devise a scheme to make these available and perhaps the proceeds could go into a fund to support education, research or support of creative endeavour. The duration of copyright is probably now too long and could be shortened to say thirty years, with the option of renewable licences. The granting of licences to reproduce copyright material should be simpler and cheaper. Private study rules should be widened and easy availability of material for all should be a realisable goal. Legal deposit is probably no longer either necessary or desirable. For the sake of future scholars, the registration and preservation of databases, websites and e-mails should be encouraged and indeed made mandatory. Piracy must not be colluded with nor should censorship be hidden under the guise of copyright control.

Yet, these are all minor and solvable issues compared to the central grandeur and immutability of the principle of Anne enacted here with the approval and support of the Stationers' Company three centuries ago. There is no more noble aim that the 'Encouragement of Learning by vesting the copies of printed books in the authors and purchasers of such copies during the times mentioned.' It is up to us as the successors of those who fought for that right to protect it and adapt it to the age of Google, the World Wide Web and Computing in the Clouds.

Is Queen Anne's Statute Relevant to Twitter?

JOHN HOWKINS

John Howkins is a leading figure in the global development of cultural and creative industries. John is Chairman of London-based BOP Consulting and a Board Director of HandMade plc,which produced the 2009 anima-tion, 'Planet 51', and of HotBed Media Ltd. He is a Director of Screen East, the UK regional screen agency.

Howkins & Associates has a joint venture with Info-Space in Beijing, is an investor in the Shanghai Creative Industries Investment Company which owns '1933' in Hongkou and is Chief Advisor to the Old Canal Develop-ment Zone, Wuxi.

John has advised numerous multinational companies, businesses, govern-ment organisations and cultural agencies and has worked in over 30 coun-tries including Australia, Canada, China, France, Greece, India, Italy, Japan, Mexico, Poland, Singapore, UK and USA.

He is the Founder and Director of the Adelphi Charter on Creativity, Inno-vation and Intellectual Property, and devised the London Intellectual Prop-erty Advisory Service ('Own It'). In 2010 he is co-organising and chairing British Council copyright forums in London and Shanghai.

He was associated with Time Warner Inc from 1982 to1996 with respon-sibilities for TV businesses in Europe. He is Deputy Chairman of the British Screen Advisory Council (BSAC). He is a Member of the United Nations Advisory Committee on the Creative Economy and a Council Member of the UK government's Arts and Humanities Research Council (AHRC). He is a former Chairman of the London Film School, Vice Chairman of the Association of Independent Producers and Executive Director of the Inter-national Institute of Communications (IIC).

He is the author of 'Communications in China', 'Four Global Scenarios for Information', 'The Creative Economy', 'CODE', 'Dutty's Dare' (with Zhao Li), 'Creative Ecologies' and other books. www.creativeeconomy.com; info@creativeeconomy.com.

Abstract: It's odd to suggest a 300 year old statute may be relevant today and doubly so in media markets where regulations change every few years. But imagine the next stage of Twitter where tweets can include sounds and pictures, and the next stage of the Internet where Google can search for objects as well as words. We need some principles to make sense of this and provide a solid basis for laws and commercial contracts. Most policy-makers would admit, if only in private, that governments lack a ready framework for understanding what is happening, and lack also in-house expertise. Information and media industries do not have an equivalent body of professional expertise or research theory that informs other areas of public policy such as agriculture, education, construction, manufacturing, defence and trade. One of the most exciting challenges of the future is how to generate such basic resources. Until then, the six principles of the 1709[1] Statute are a good place to start.

Is Queen Anne's Statute relevant to Twitter?

Does a 300-year-old law which few people have read matter at all? Most laws over 50 years old are a bit dusty. Media regulations need to be changed every few years. Maybe the Queen Anne statute is irrelevant.

The most important ideas about copyright in recent years did not come from any rights-holder. They did not originate in any publication, think-tank, national government or WIPO but in a California-based company, in between the Pacific mountains and the southern reaches of San Francisco Bay, which wants to make books more easily available online. The smart guys at Google want to make it easier for us to find and read books. They think it would bring more traffic to their site, cut readers' costs and is an all-round neat idea.

The US Department of Justice listened to rights-holders and was unconvinced. Several European governments, including France and Germany, protested. Virtually all politicians, and many authors, publishers and book-sellers, are confused. Some authors echo the feelings of Jack Valenti, President of Hollywood's MPAA, when he attacked the video recorder, 'I say to you that the VCR is to the Amer-

---

[1]   In 1709 the Statute of Anne, "An Act for the Encouragement of Learning by vesting the Copies of Printed Books in the Authors or purchasers of such Copies, during the Times therein mentioned".

ican film producer and the American public as the Boston strangler is to the woman home alone.'

Why did this happen? Why is publishing being re-invented by a company that has never published a book in its life and has little sympathy with the ink-and-paper business?

Rights-holders fear Google will undercut their copyright-based business model of maximising revenues by restricting the sale of rights. It's a good model and still works well for business-to-business deals, although cracks in the foundation are beginning to show. For hundreds of years it has enabled media investors to cover the costs of financing expensive books, albums, films and TV programmes, as well as enabling manufacturers to develop ever more sophisticated copying technologies (like the VCR and DVD). As a result of this long boom, market demand for media entertainment is higher than ever. Hollywood reported a 8% increase in box office revenues in 2009, and the UK, dependent on US films, also did well. The numbers of British book titles reached new records in 2009. According to the IFPI, UK music sales increased in 2009 although global sales were down by 7%.

Media owners are also discovering the importance of differential pricing. Someone wanting an out-of-copyright 'Jane Eyre' and a new bestseller from Martin Amis or Stieg Larsson, or choosing between a ticket to a £500,000 budget movie and £450 million Hollywood movie, has traditionally been asked to pay about the same price. That's now changed. A ticket to see 'Avatar' in 3D costs about 30-40% more than the 2D version (most people who have seen both versions say the premium is worth it). The film distributors who sell rights to 2D screens, 3D screens, IMAX, pay-TV, Video-on-Demand and DVD are seeing retail prices vary from £2-3 to a top of £30. The digital systems that make this possible started in America and Europe but are having a dramatic effect in Africa and Asia, including China.

Copyright has played a small role in these changes by facilitating business-to-business deals. But the chief causes have been new technology and new regulations. New technology, both analog and digital, has allowed more companies to provide competitive services. In turn, governments have abolished monopolies and allowed outsiders to compete on equal terms and to offer more consumer choice. Book publishers who were immune from commercial pressures for a long time (helped by the net book agreement) suddenly found themselves having to fight for attention.

Even without the Internet, media companies, backed by governments, have enabled consumers to enjoy a breath-taking expansion of media experiences, from a hundred CD versions of classic compositions to Sky's 600+ channels to 3D movies.

With the Internet, the expansion is virtually infinite. The Internet is the world's most wonderful device for accessing and sharing and facilitates an explosion of copying. People who say the Internet is as big as Gutenberg's development of printing miss the point. It is as if Gutenberg invented printing, film, TV, photocopying, computers and optical disc recording one giddy morning and then drew back the curtains on globalisation after lunch.

With such a bonanza, it is not surprising that the old division between experiencing, ownership, borrowing and outright theft have become a trifle fuzzy. Most copying is legal because the rights-holder wants the stuff to be copied. But some is illegal, because the rights-holder wants income.

Boundaries get fuzzier every year

The boundaries get fuzzier every year. Google Books is the first of a new wave of initiatives. Tim Berners-Lee is pursuing the vision of a 'semantic web' which allows computers to comprehend the meaning of software and to search and sort for semantic relationships (it's fair to say quite a few people are sceptical). The Internet of Things has many more supporters including major US, German and Chinese companies, strongly backed by their governments. This links the power of search machines and the Radio Frequency Identification (RFID) electronic tags that manufacturers are increasingly embedding in manufactured objects, notably clothing and household goods as well as packaged food, to allow them to track its movements from the factory to the shop (and why stop there?). So while at present we use a search machine to find web pages with the words we are looking for, the semantic web will allow us to find a web page with the meanings we want, and the Internet of Things will allow us to find the object we want. Type in 'socks, red, lost', and Google or Baidu or whatever your favoured machine is will flash up, "right behind you, just where you thought they were."

Meanwhile software companies are working out how to extend Twitter's 140-letter capacity and how it can send sounds and pictures. Twitter's 140 character limit is surely part of its charm but the urge to expand is irresistible. After all, as Adam Singer, Chairman of the British Screen Advisory Council says, the only difference between text and music and pictures is bandwidth.

Who owns the copyright in a tweet or a video tweet?

We can only make sense of this creative ecology by re-thinking the fundamentals of copyright, and, indeed, of all the rules and regulations that affect how we share and get access to media content and information. It's not just copyright. The debate on information access, which is what we are really talking about, involves confidentiality, privacy, personal data rights, competition policy and, in some countries, human rights legislation. At one extreme, it involves plagiarism; at another free speech.

Governments' piecemeal approach

The piecemeal approach favoured by most governments, such as keeping the definition of qualifying works but fiddling with copyright exemptions, or changing term durations but not changing market access rules, will soon be overtaken by technology and may lose consumer credibility. This may seem a tall order, but let's remember the Queen Anne statute really started life as a competition policy initiative.

We can see the emergence of three kinds of licensing: (1) fully commercial, restricted licensing which is necessary to enable investors and producers to make commercial, large-scale media productions; (2) non-commercial but still restricted licences for people who want to share their work but want to retain some rights such as moral rights and commercial derivative uses (typically, Creative Commons) and (3) non-commercial and non-restrictive licences for people who want their work to have as wide usage as possible and don't want to retain any control over it (such as user-generated, social media).

Trying to maintain the same laws and licences over a £100 million movie, a book edition costing £50,000 and a YouTube video is doomed to failure. If the English MPs of 1709 had been faced with a similar range of activities, I doubt they would have been so ambitious or so foolhardy.

The 1709 Statute on Copyright revealed its extraordinary quality in its headline: "An Act for the Encouragement of Learning." In my work on the creative ecology it has become clear that learning is the most common and probably the most critical characteristic of creative people, from the genius to the journeyman. Creative people may differ in everything else but they are all persistent learners.

Parliament was reflecting the mood of the times. Isaac Newton who had been a Member of Parliament a few years earlier (it is absurd to imagine such a world-ranking scientist being a member of Britain's parliament today) said that he had managed to develop the concept of gravity "by standing on the shoulders of giants," a phrase he himself had borrowed from earlier writers. The purpose of the 1709 Statute was to enable the giants to stay standing while making it possible for others to look even further ahead.

Statute covers most of today's issues

The statute covers most of today's issues – including ethics, free speech, ownership, fair competition, money, theft and the public domain. It established six principles:

1. The purpose of the 'encouragement of learning' (repeated verbatim in the 1790 USA Copyright Act).
2. The right of authors to own their output.
3. The right of the public to access what is written.
4. The principle that both these rights are conditional.
5. The principle that both rights should be mutually balanced.
6. The principle that the terms of trade between authors and printers/publishers should be fair.

Given today's cornucopia, rather than assert private ownership and then allow a few exemptions, perhaps we need to assert public use and then allow a few commercial exemptions.

No one would argue that Mickey Mouse should never be in copyright (if so, Walt Disney could not have paid his rent). However, nobody would argue that the person who invented Mickey should have total control over his name (otherwise I could not quote him in this article).

Where, though, should we draw the line? What is the right way to regulate the ownership of ideas in the twenty-first century? There is the belief that we have a basic, permanent right to our ideas and that we have a right to charge others compensation if they want to use our ideas. In such a world, incentives and rewards take priority and always trump access. There is a second purpose which some people find counter-intuitive. The laws also enable people to have access to what has been created. This puts access above incentives and rewards.

Which is the best way forward? I want to suggest an answer based on the creative ecology and the individual's freedom to make their ideas central to their lives; to use their ideas to build up their own personality, identity and status; to use their ideas to build up their earning power; and to turn these assets into their own creative capital.

There are three concentric spheres of creativity. First, there is the commercial world which requires substantial, long-term investments and a robust revenue stream. The author's creative processes have not changed much in 300 years but the potential for exploitation has exploded. Even so, commercial authors are a small minority. A larger number of people are willing for others to use their work for non-commercial purposes. And countless people are exploring ideas, sounds, and images, and are creating work with no thought of its commercial value or, to be more precise, of claiming any exclusive rights over it.

Today, creativity is not the exclusive preserve of a few exceptional people but the result of millions of people, often working freely and collaboratively. The pursuit of learning, as indeed the pursuit of happiness, often depends upon one's freedom to pursue one's own ideas. This dynamic operates differently in various cultures. I spend several months in China every year where I am acutely aware of the differences between the eighteenth-century Enlightenment traditions that are dominant in Europe and America and the older Asian traditions of social harmony that are prevalent in China. Each exemplifies a different way of using ideas and knowledge.

It is clear to me that a country's "encouragement of learning" is just as important, if not more so, as its encouragement of trade in commodities, manufactures and financial services. Actually, of course, they are mutually interdependent.

I take away three or four points from these anniversary discussions. Copyright is only one of a whole matrix of regulatory mechanisms. It started as a device to encourage learning by means of ensuring fair competition and fair terms of trade between two groups of people and it abandons that role at its peril. We need to rethink where copyright is essential and where it is a hindrance. Queen Anne's six principles are not a bad place to start.

How can Government meet the Challenges of Balancing Effective Copyright Protection in the Digital Age against the Needs of Users?

JUDITH SULLIVAN

After graduating in natural sciences from Cambridge University, Judith Sullivan worked in the research department at Glaxo Pharmaceuticals, and then later became a patent examiner. In 1984/5 and then from the early 1990s until 2005, she was part of the directorate developing intellectual property policy for the UK Government. Much of that time was spent in the copyright policy making team, which she ultimately led before leaving to become an independent copyright consultant. She was involved in developing copyright policy on a number of issues, including copyright enforcement, new exceptions benefitting visually impaired people and UK implementation of the 2001 EU copyright Directive. As a copyright consultant she has, in particular, written a study for WIPO on copyright exceptions and visually impaired people, worked for the British Screen Advisory Council on a number of copyright issues and, more recently, provided policy advice to the States of Jersey on updating its copyright law.

Abstract: Taking as the starting point that a legal framework must encourage creativity to flourish, the paper explores a former copyright policy makers' perspective of the frustrations in identifying and delivering a balance between the interests of all stakeholders. It looks at the failure to legalise private copying in the past and the difficulties involved in doing that in the digital world when individuals wish, not only to copy things for themselves, but also make mash-ups and share content on the internet. Education about copyright and enforcement against illegal use are unlikely to stop people wanting to do these things and so changes are probably needed to legalise what people want to do with appropriate royalty payments. Legislative change tends to be complicated, but voluntary measures can also be part of any solution. The paper goes on to explore how the issue of "private" copying is part of a wider debate, which probably needs to take place at international level, about copyright conferring exclusive rights or merely providing a right to remuneration. Moral rights and the term of protection may also be relevant to this debate. It concludes that policy makers need to mediate between stakeholders to gain acceptance for policy changes.

How can government meet the challenges of balancing effective copyright protection in the digital age against the needs of users?

This paper draws on about 20 years, on and off, in copyright policy making for the UK Government, but I have tried to use that experience to look at the future rather than just dwell on the past. Indeed, I am not at liberty to talk freely about the past, but I will mention a couple of things that are common knowledge to illustrate the type of frustrations that policy makers surely still face.

Policy making needs to deliver a legal framework that encourages creativity to flourish, by permitting those who create and invest in creativity to obtain a reward. A common misunderstanding, in my experience, is the belief that copyright policy makers must therefore support copyright owners more than other stakeholders. But policy makers must always have regard to the wider public interest. The material that might be created because of the promise of rewards from exercising exclusive rights can clearly benefit everyone, because it is enjoyed for entertainment, used in education and so on, but there may also be public interest reasons to constrain or curtail rights. The overriding strategy for those determining the policy in the area of copyright is to strive for an appropriate balance between the interests of all stakeholders.

A good historical example of the frustration involved in determining that balance relates to the issue of private copying. The failure, at the time UK copyright law was updated in 1988, to make any change to the law which addressed the ease of copying music onto tapes, and the public's increasing desire to do that, is well known. A blank tape levy had been proposed, coupled with making the copying legal, but that didn't happen because of the difficulties of making such a levy fair. Doing nothing, and so simply leaving the private copying illegal, was perhaps the easiest option politically, but doing nothing has certainly left unfinished business, although things have, of course, moved on from recording music onto tapes.

The second example from the past is the restrictions on new exceptions in the 2001 EU copyright Directive. That Directive was the culmination of very difficult and lengthy negotiations, and the end result is, of course, an inevitable compromise. Much in the Directive was good for the UK, such as the recognition that dissemination of works on the internet must be something that copyright owners can be rewarded for. Arguably this was just bringing the EU up to the standards that those drafting the UK legislation in 1988 had cleverly, or fortuitously, anticipated! But the Directive came with various warts, such as constraining provision on exceptions to rights. The fact that the possibility of making provision for use of orphan works by an exception is now an EU issue does limit the UK's options for solving problems.

These examples illustrate some difficulties with policy making. There tends to be an inbuilt inertia because of the challenge involved in isolating the true problems from much biased special pleading and identifying fair solutions. And at the European and international levels, the UK's proud tradition of 300 years of copyright law certainly does not give it any special entitlement to see things done the way it thinks is best. It is also true that policy developed in haste as a result of special pleading is unlikely to make good law in the copyright area anymore than it does in other areas. When the final, generally pragmatic, policy solution eventually emerges, it is likely to please no-one, so the special pleading starts all over again.

Private copying continues to be a big, unresolved policy issue in the digital age and policy makers have quite rightly been thinking about possible policy changes. In the digital world, private copying has, of course, become a lot more complicated. What starts as some limited private copying can so often lead to sharing with others, including putting copies on the internet. What users can do easily is likely to always be difficult to stop. There is no 300 year history of enormous respect for copyright law which makes the very existence of copyright something that inhibits people. It's just that for most of those years any significant amount of copying and sharing required so much investment that ordinary people weren't particularly tempted. So, for policy makers now, there is the well-recognised challenge of either getting people to understand and respect the boundaries imposed by copyright law, enforcing the law against potentially a very large number of people, changing the law so the boundaries fall where most people naturally comply with it, encouraging rights owners, collaborating as necessary with others, to voluntarily do something that solves all the problems, or doing some of all of these.

Pragmatic policy makers probably back the last of these. Better education about copyright has been an agenda item for many years now, but is unlikely to solve everything. Enforcement against P2P file sharing may be made more effective by the action to be required of ISPs in the current Digital Economy Bill that is wending its way through Parliament as I write, but that won't necessarily stop people from wanting to share or to put their mash-ups on You-Tube. Changes are therefore probably needed, but deciding whether these should be legal ones or voluntary ones, and trying to obtain a consensus about what the changes might be, is difficult. Of course, changing the law does not have to be merely a matter of legalising more things only. It can also be about when, and if so, how, any legalised copying beyond a certain point leads to a royalty payment. And that sort of solution can potentially be delivered voluntarily by right holders making it easy to license what people want to do. This is therefore the modern debate about levies, but I doubt that levies in the traditional sense can solve everything, and maybe, as the UK IPO has recognised, the debate cannot be confined to the UK alone.

The blank tape levy was perhaps a great idea as a policy solution for private copying in its time, and it seems to have worked fine in a number of countries. But users in the UK were perhaps more organised than in those countries, and so were able to win their argument about a levy being unfair to those, particularly visually impaired people, not infringing copyright when using tapes. And the increasing number of things on which a levy might be paid, including things that a particular person might use exclusively in ways where no copyright material is copied, certainly calls into question the sustainability of this solution. What needs to be covered by a new "great idea" to address expanded "private" copying has been debated by many – as well as copying for things like format shifting, it may need to incorporate a right to quote from, mash up and share protected material. But how legislative and/or voluntary solutions might deliver this, and when and how royalties should be paid, is not easily determined.

A legislative solution is bound to be difficult. The starting point is the constraints in international treaties on the extent to which right holders can have their right to say "no" taken away, and there are numerous factors to consider here. As my first boss said to me, when I knew very little about copyright, the devil is in the detail. Too true, and despite protestations from some that copyright is too complicated, the detail seems to still reign supreme. Witness for example the growing complexity of the provision on orphan works in the Digital Economy Bill. And this does not even include the regulations that will be needed before anything is actually implemented.

So, for example, in a legislative solution on private copying, sharing and so on, would it be fair to permit this for something that you only got via a streamed service, or one where you can keep the copy for a short time only (online "rental"), or must you first of all have a copy that you are entitled to keep permanently? How can royalties be collected, rates decided and so on? And will it be necessary to exclude from any royalty payment uses that perhaps ought to be totally free, such as limited use for criticism or review?

"Private" copying is, of course, part of a wider debate on copyright conferring exclusive rights or merely a right to remuneration. There are many other users of copyright material as well as the private individual. For example, there are libraries and education, those wanting to offer content services, and those such as broadcasters, producers and publishers who are both right holders and users. A right to say "no" may be argued by authors as being essential in order to stop use of their material in ways they deem unacceptable, but when should they be able to stop use and when should they just be entitled to remuneration? And can moral rights be part of any solution, for example by adding a new moral right regarding certain types of objectionable associations to the existing right to object to derogatory treatment of the work? A right to say "no" may be argued by investors as crucial in order to be able to control, and so maximise the revenue from, the first exposure of the material to the public in various ways, but does this argument really justify a right to say "no" for the entire term of copyright?

Of course, possible changes to the term of copyright can be debated too, and a key issue here may be the extent to which copyright for one thing can be justified because it leads to revenue that can be invested in creating another thing, which may itself never be successful? Debates about copyright do not always seem to acknowledge the potential difference in how a policy issue might be decided when looking at copyright as a reward for creativity, that is facilitating payments for the time spent creating in the past, as opposed to copyright which raises money to invest in creating something else in the future. The issues that would need to be debated here have certainly now strayed into areas where EU and international law do not permit the UK to unilaterally change anything.

I have probably adopted the usual policy maker's approach in writing this paper, namely to plagiarise any good ideas. I can only apologise for this and ask that everyone feel acknowledged as necessary. I also no longer have any responsibility for making policy in the UK, so nothing in this paper need constrain the policy makers.

Indeed, my work in the last few years as a consultant has given me the opportunity to understand the position of certain stakeholders better, but I may therefore also be less balanced than I was in understanding the issues!

So, to conclude, deciding what is in the public interest in any area is hard and copyright policy is no exception. For example, it may be in the public interest to remove any copyright constraints where excerpts of content need to be used for news reporting, but beware, say, lobbying from people claiming a "public interest" in removing all copyright constraints from someone who wants to circulate the last chapter of a top-selling book just because the public are interested! Policy makers must ultimately distinguish reasonable concerns from indefensible claims in order to identify fair policy solutions. And gaining acceptance for any policy, as well as encouraging effective voluntary solutions to emerge, can be facilitated by both public and private mediation between stakeholders, so that different interests truly appreciate each others' perspectives. A good policy decision may then be one that no-one is completely happy about, but hopefully it is one where everyone can see that they were at least listened to.